DAILY DOSES OF WISDOM

Daily Doses
of Wisdom

A Year of
Buddhist
Inspiration

EDITED BY Josh Bartok

WISDOM PUBLICATIONS · BOSTON

Wisdom Publications
199 Elm Street
Somerville, MA 02144 USA
www.wisdompubs.org

Library of Congress Cataloging-in-Publication Data

Daily doses of wisdom : a year of Buddhist inspiration / edited by Josh Bartok.
    pages cm
Includes bibliographical references and index.
ISBN 1-61429-111-X (pbk. : alk. paper)
1. Buddhist devotional calendars. 2. Buddhist meditations. I. Bartok, Josh,
editor of compilation.
 BQ5579.D33 2013
 294.3'4432—dc22

                              2013004725

ISBN 978-1-61429-111-4   eBook ISBN 978-1-61429-132-9

17 16 15 14 13   5 4 3 2 1

Cover design by Phil Pascuzzo. Interior design by Gopa&Ted2, Inc.
Set in Mr. Eaves San OT 12/16.2.

Wisdom Publications' books are printed on acid-free paper and meet
the guidelines for permanence and durability of the Production Guidelines
for Book Longevity of the Council on Library Resources.

Printed in the United States of America.

For Liz Roemer,
with love and gratitude.

Publisher's Acknowledgment

The publisher gratefully acknowledges the generous contribution of the Hershey Family Foundation toward the publication of this book.

Table of Contents

Preface

Shakyamuni Buddha is often called the Great Physician, and the liberating medicine he offers us is his teaching. Similarly, the bodhisattva of compassion holds out a medicine jar; she responds with breaking heart to the cries of the world by dispensing the healing balm of Dharma. How lucky are we all to be under the care of such transcendently skilled healthcare professionals! "Steeped in luck," as the poet Seamus Heaney says, "steeped, steeped, steeped in luck."

For each of the 365 entries here, we can imagine the Buddha himself, Guanyin herself, lovingly offering us a single luminous spoonful of wisdom—the exact dose we need to meet our day a little more choicefully, to take one step closer to being the person we aspire to be, to find just a little more freedom right here amid the fires of being human. You might want to receive this treatment before you sit down to meditate or as you stand up from your cushion, before you go to sleep or right after you wake up. Indeed, there is no wrong time for the Dharma and no wrong amount—truly the Dharma is, as the Buddha says, "good in the beginning, good in the middle, and good in the end."

Please enjoy *Daily Doses of Wisdom*—let this book and the teachings in it be part of the way you appreciate your life and care for all beings.

The process of bringing any book into being makes clear just how interdependently connected we all are—and how much more so a book like this, distilled from so many sources, so many teachers, so many bodhisattvas. Each of Wisdom's authors and all of Wisdom's books have become teachers to me, companions and trusted friends to me on my own Dharma path—and I offer a deep bow to each of you. After almost thirteen years editing Dharma books for Wisdom Publications, I don't really feel I can adequately express the depth of appreciation for this great gift.

Even so: Tim McNeill, Wisdom's publisher—thank you for this opportunity, thank you for your trust and support these many years, and thank you for sustaining Wisdom for so long in the service of so many. David Kittelstrom, thanks for first opening the door for me. I also especially want to thank Laura Cunningham—thank you for doing so much so cheerfully for this book (and many others!). I want to offer appreciation as well to the incomparable Phil Pascuzzo for the magnificently perfect cover design, and Gopa&Ted2 for yet another lovely interior. And finally, I offer thanks also to all my colleagues at Wisdom—present and former (I'm looking at you, Rod Meade Sperry!)—who are working to save all beings, one great Dharma book at a time.

Borrowing words from Zen Master Dogen, let me conclude by saying this: "Please treasure yourself."

—JOSH BARTOK,
Greater Boston Zen Center, Cambridge, Massachusetts

I

There is nothing magical about meditation.

———

Meditation is bound to fail if it is being done to fix a problem.

———

Don't meditate to fix yourself, to heal yourself, to improve yourself, to redeem yourself; rather, do it as an act of love, of deep warm friendship toward yourself. In this view there is no longer any need for the subtle aggression of self-improvement, for self-criticism, for the endless guilt of not doing enough. It offers the possibility of an end to the ceaseless round of trying so hard that wraps so many people's lives in a knot. Instead there is now meditation as an act of love. How endlessly delightful and encouraging!

—Bob Sharples,
Meditation and Relaxation in Plain English

2

According to a Hindu myth, the world is upheld by the great elephant Maha Pudma, who is in turn supported by the great tortoise Chukwa.

An Englishman asked a Hindu sage what the great tortoise rests upon.

"Another turtle," was the reply.

And what supports that turtle?

"Ah, Sahib, after that it's turtles all the way down."

—FROM *The World Is Made of Stories*

3

Use your own problems to remember that others have problems too.

—Kathleen McDonald,
Awakening the Kind Heart

4

Successful spiritual development entails finding a balance between intellectual understanding of each stage of meditation and actual meditative experience. Placing too much emphasis on either alone significantly decreases the likelihood of genuine progress.

—DANIEL P. BROWN,
Pointing Out the Great Way

5

Be at ease. Be still. Be vigilant. These three qualities of the body are to be maintained throughout all meditation sessions.

—B. ALAN WALLACE,
The Attention Revolution

6

Although it is difficult to bring about the inner change that gives rise to compassion, it is absolutely worthwhile to try.

—THE DALAI LAMA
IN *Business and the Buddha*

7

At first glance the Buddhist insight into impermanence may not seem too remarkable. Surely every tradition recognizes and appreciates change. What is unique to the Buddhist view is the radical extension of change to *all phenomena whatsoever*. We are used to hearing that some things change, or even that most things change, but it is profoundly challenging to hear that all things change. There is no unchanging essence underlying the effervescent bubbling of our minds and bodies; no unmoved mover standing outside the matrix of cause and effect; no fixed point upon which one can find firm footing; no refuge from the relentless onslaught of aging, illness, and death. We can of course conjure up a concept or an idea of such a stable essence but we cannot, says the Buddha, ever discover it in carefully examined lived experience. We cannot even hold the idea of something stable for long in the shifting currents of the mind.

Indeed the mind itself is the most dramatic example of thoroughgoing change. The very tool we use to construct a world of meaning is itself wobbling, so it is no surprise that we build with it a wobbling world.

➥

By identifying impermanence as a fundamental *characteristic* of existence itself, rather than a *problem* to be solved, the Buddhists are encouraging us to let go our hold on illusory solidity and learn to swim freely in the sea of change. Instead of mourning what is lost when alteration occurs, we can open to the opportunities each new moment brings.

—ANDREW OLENDZKI,
Unlimiting Mind

8

Your mind is birthless and continuous,
without a beginning, middle, or end.

The rising and sinking of agitated waves
ceases by itself without interference.
This mind that is obscured by thoughts,
when left as it is, unmodified, will clarify as the
   dharmakaya.

Do not modify it, but rest in relaxation.
Do not control the mind, but let it go free.
Do not have intentions, but be spacious.
Do not focus on anything, but be expansive.

—LAMA SHANG
IN *Mahamudra and Related Instructions*

9

Many of us began spiritual practice as a means of resolving trauma. Unfortunately, the image of the unattached, enlightened, fierce Zen master who has transcended self-clinging and happily lives the hermit's life, appealing as it is, may not be so useful. We need to integrate meditation's energetic awareness into our personal traumas, our wounds, and our defense mechanisms. Zen practice means finding the mind of meditation in times of fear, anger, and desire, rather than trying to banish fear, anger, and desire from our consciousness. We need to practice what we preach in intimate relationships that affect us on a daily basis. This dimension of practice is not well articulated in the stories that present male ancestors as masters who have completely transcended human needs, but it is addressed repeatedly in the lives and teachings of female ancestors.

—GRACE SCHIRESON,
Zen Women

10

It's not by gathering causes
    that an unconditioned result
    will be reached;

it's not by looking for freedom
    that freedom
    will be found.

—CHARLES GENOUD,
Gesture of Awareness

II

Disillusionment is always painful—but it can be deeply valuable as well. Disillusionment is, after all, our growing out of illusion and into reality—i.e., how things are versus how we wish or imagine them to be. To a large degree, becoming disillusioned equals growing up.

—SCOTT EDELSTEIN,
Sex and the Spiritual Teacher

12

Open your heart to your suffering. If you're feeling that family and friends could be helping more but aren't, take compassionate action toward yourself by immediately making contact with them. Often people are just waiting to be asked to help but won't make that first contact.

—TONI BERNHARD,
How to Be Sick

13

What is the use of a well
if water is all around?
If the root of thirst is cut,
what can one go and search for?

—FROM *Divine Stories*

14

I'm thankful for being given the opportunity to love and be
loved by others, and to express that love through service.
The little good I do in this world is, truly, the least I can do
in return, but it is what I can do.

—JEFF WILSON,
Buddhism of the Heart

15

One of the first signs of progress in practice is simply noticing how chaotic our minds are. We try to remain attentive, but we swiftly "lose our minds" and slip into absent-mindedness. People who never sit quietly and try to focus their minds may remain under the illusion that their minds are calm and collected. Only when we try to direct the attention to a single object for minutes on end does it really become apparent how turbulent and fragmented our attention is.

———

Thoughts are bound to arise involuntarily, and your attention may also be pulled away by noises and other stimuli from your environment. When you note that you have become distracted, instead of tightening up and forcing your attention back to the breath, simply let go of these thoughts and distractions. Especially with each out-breath, relax your body, release extraneous thoughts, and happily let your attention settle back into the body. When you see that your mind has wandered, don't get upset. Just be happy that you've noticed the distraction and gently return to the breath.

—B. ALAN WALLACE,
The Attention Revolution

16

It doesn't take any great wisdom to know that until you stop doing something, you're still doing it. As long as you keep on lying, you're a liar. Until you stop killing, you're a killer. And there's no guarantee that just because *you've* stopped others will stop too. Inclusion makes one vulnerable. This is the cost that mercy exacts of the merciful.

—

Surely if the Buddha could open his heart to the very one who'd come seeking his death, I should be able to find some degree of understanding and compassion for those who might threaten me with harm. It's an unfortunate habit of the human mind to take sides, dividing up society on the basis of arbitrary standards. It's a persistent habit that insinuates itself into language and spreads its influence by that means to others. To the degree that it's a habit of my own behavior, I'm determined to stop. Perhaps, if I succeed, others will be encouraged to stop too.

—Lin Jensen,
Together Under One Roof

17

When I ask someone what his or her practice is, I'll usually be told something like "counting my breaths." But what is that person really doing? Whatever method of meditation we adopt, we are inevitably going to try to enlist that practice in the service of one or more of our *curative fantasies*. A curative fantasy is a personal myth that we use to explain what we think is wrong with us and our lives and what we imagine is going to make it all better. Sometimes these fantasies are quite explicit: we're sure we know what's wrong and we're sure we know what we're after. Curative fantasies take many forms, and when you know where to look, they can be seen in all sorts of places.

—

The fundamental dualism we face on the cushion is not some metaphysical abstraction, it is the all too down-to-earth experience of a person divided against herself in the pursuit of a curative fantasy.

—BARRY MAGID,
Ending the Pursuit of Happiness

18

Even if its impact isn't immediate, a solid inner change is sure to have longterm results.

—THANISSARO BHIKKHU
IN *Mindful Politics*

19

The truly religious life liberates a finite, relative being to become a "rare and excellent person" naturally and spontaneously. As imperfect humans, we are bound by our karmic limitations, but that poses no hindrance for reflecting the boundless life and light of the Buddha. It is not the case that everything that karmic evil connotes, including human foolishness, frailties, and failures, completely vanish—but that the overwhelming working of compassion nullifies their negative karmic impact, enabling limited beings to make unlimited contributions to the well-being of all life.

—TAITETSU UNNO
IN *Buddhism and Psychotherapy Across Cultures*

20

Becoming aware of death, our natural reaction is to recoil from it, deny it, hide from it. Instead of embracing our full reality, we tend to attribute permanence, substance, and unchangingness to constructs that cannot live up to these qualities. We cling to loved ones and to our own lives, desperately wanting them to be everlasting. But if we are instead lucky enough to find within ourselves a seed of what motivated Prince Siddhartha two and a half millennia ago, we might begin to investigate what the alternative to clinging is.

—

The way to wisdom is to hold all things, including ourselves, in open hands. In this difficult but necessary way, we discover how we can return to our authentic heritage, our true home. We can learn to use the fire of our minds to good purpose.

—JAMES ISHMAEL FORD,
Zen Master WHO?

21

Difficult people can teach us patience.

If we are sincere about working on ourselves—decreasing our ego, anger, and other delusions, and increasing patience, love, and other positive qualities—then someone who arouses our anger is like a teacher, giving us a chance to learn that we still have a lot of work to do. Think of a time when difficulties with another person taught you important lessons. Resolve that when you again encounter problems with people, you will use these as opportunities for growth. It's possible that you may end up feeling grateful for the difficult people in your life!

—KATHLEEN MCDONALD,
Awakening the Kind Heart

22

The word *meditation* in the modern world often has the connotation of doing something special to calm the mind or try to achieve some altered state of consciousness. But the Sanskrit word for meditation is *bhavana*, which simply means "cultivation." In fact, we are all cultivating our minds in one way or another all the time, through the way we use our attention. The quality of our lives reflects the ways we have cultivated our minds until now.

—B. Alan Wallace,
The Attention Revolution

23

One of the great losses in our modern secular world is the absence of ritual. Ritual helps to make an activity feel special, and it provides a bridge between the mundane world of ordinary reality and the possibility of a spiritual or transcendent reality. To practice meditation is to be a little more open to the spiritual and the numinous. Many people find it helpful to use a ritual as an entry point into their meditation. The ritual serves to remind them that this is a special time, a time they are setting aside for their inner life, for spiritual practice, for healing, or simply for rest and renewal.

—BOB SHARPLES,
Meditation and Relaxation in Plain English

24

You cannot make your body flexible just by thinking about making it flexible. You can only do that by training it; the *body* has to make the body flexible. Just as physical flexibility has to be created by our body, mental flexibility—which is another name for ultimate peace and happiness—has to be created by our mind, through mental training. Meditation is mental training.

—LAMA ZOPA RINPOCHE,
How to Be Happy

25

This path leads us to a life where we can truly meet each event, each person, each thing intimately and directly. This intimate directness has no hesitation in it. We perceive clearly, and we move or stay still according to circumstances.

—MELISSA MYOZEN BLACKER,
The Book of Mu

26

By just sitting without expectation, the natural stability and clarity of my mind gradually strengthens, little by little. Then I am able to turn that mind upon itself and inquire, "Who? What? Where is that mind?" Not finding anything brings further giving up and a little bit of relaxation in genuineness. With this comes a small further step in understanding the truths of basic goodness, the cocoon by which I cover them, and the way out of the cocoon to realize that basic goodness, our inherent nature of wisdom.

—JEREMY HAYWARD,
Warrior-King of Shambhala

27

Whatever your path at this moment, every single step is equal in substance. Every step actualizes the true self. Every moment of practice is always the koan of having to agree to your condition, to bring unlimited friendliness to what you are, just as you are, right now. Even your obnoxiousness, your failures, your rank inadequacy is it. Your best revenge is to include it as you.

—SUSAN MURPHY,
Upside-Down Zen

28

Our highest aspirations, like the highest tips of the tallest trees, must of necessity remain rooted in the ground below. It's natural to look upward as well as down, to reach for the heavens while depending on the earth. We humans live a seesaw sort of life, going up only to come down again, going down in order to push back up. It's an intricate cooperation between rise and descent, and, while the going up is good and the heights are grand, it's essential to come back to earth again, back to our roots.

—LIN JENSEN,
Deep Down Things

29

In addition to compassion, I found that patience is key to understanding how fear affects us. Usually we refuse to experience fear. We try either to get rid of it or immediately resolve the situation that triggers it. So with patience, we can witness the mind running through its reactive, patterned responses to fear.

At the beginning of a long retreat some years ago, Ajahn Sumedho said in one of his teachings, "If you think you have a problem with fear, you will keep recreating fear." I had been struggling with fear for weeks, and as he said this, I understood how much I had identified with fear as "my problem."

So I vowed that if fear arose, however convincing it might seem, I would not try to resolve it, to "let it go," or to do anything but simply be aware of it. By the end of the retreat, as the fear came and went, my heart was at peace with it. The anticipation, aversion, and desire to control it had been the real causes of suffering, not the fear itself. This was when I learned the importance of patience in uncovering all the layers at the root of my fear.

Of course the fear is there; this body is a fear body. The fear comes back but not in the same way.

—Ajahn Sundara
in *The Best of Inquiring Mind*

30

This true nature of the mind, the seed of everything,
primordially identical with the minds of all conquerors
    and their children,
is present as the birthless dharmakaya.
It is immaterial, self-knowing, and self-illuminating.
It is not a thing: It has no color, shape, or size.
It isn't nothing: Through conditions, it appears as
    everything.
It isn't permanent: It is empty by nature.
It isn't nonexistent: Its nature is unchanging
    self-illumination.
It is not a self: When examined, it has no essence.
It is not selfless: It is the great selfhood of freedom from
    elaboration.
It is not the extremes: It has no fixation whatsoever.
It is not the middle way: It is devoid of all dependency.
It cannot be identified by an example's names and
    symbols.
It has no example: It is like space.
It is not words: It cannot be described by speech.
It is not wordless: It is the cause of all expressions.

➥

It cannot be reached through words such as
existence and nonexistence, truth and falsity,
empty and not empty, peace and no peace,
elaborated and unelaborated,
conceivable and inconceivable,
happiness and suffering, perceivable and unperceivable,
dual and nondual, beyond the intellect and not beyond
    the intellect,
devoid and not devoid, existent and nonexistent,
pure and impure, naturally present and not naturally
    present.

—LAMA SHANG
IN *Mahamudra and Related Instructions*

3I

Three different epistemological approaches:
    seeing ultimate truth by way of not seeing it;
    seeing ultimate truth by transcending conceptual
        elaborations; and
    seeing ultimate truth nondually.

—SONAM THAKCHOE,
The Two Truths Debate

32

A great insight of the Buddhist tradition is the inevitable unsatisfactoriness of human experience. Often misconstrued as pessimism or even nihilism, the first noble truth—of suffering—does not deny the experience of pleasure, great joy, or happiness. Nor does it suggest that our lives are not meaningful or worthwhile. Rather it indicates a penetrating examination of the mechanisms of pleasure and happiness, and exposes an inherent limitation in the way our mind/body apparatus naturally constructs experience. Recognizing the unsatisfactoriness of our situation is a natural consequence of seeing the radical impermanence of it all.

—ANDREW OLENDZKI,
Unlimiting Mind

33

Do not turn the gods into demons.

When displeased, the worldly gods cause harm. The gods are supposed to be beneficial in general; so if they cause harm, they then become demons. Similarly, mind training is supposed to subdue self-grasping. Avoid, therefore, becoming inflated by its practice and generating conceited thoughts such as, "I am an excellent practitioner of mind training; others lack this spiritual practice." Avoid ridiculing and insulting others out of a sense of superiority. If you strengthen your grasping at the self-existence of phenomena, your practice becomes an endeavor of the enemy. It becomes the act of allowing a thief to escape into the forest while tracking his footprints on a rocky mountain. Avoid all such conduct, and by defaming self-grasping, ensure that the medicine is applied right where the illness is. Comport yourself as the lowest of the low among the servants of all sentient beings.

—SE CHILBU CHOKYI GYALTSEN
IN *Essential Mind Training*

34

Seeking the Buddha within can lead some to awakening, though it is a hard road. My concern is that this path is so frequently misconstrued and that most of us don't need stories that inspire confidence so much as ones that engender humility. Most of us are part of a cult of individuality, and a dangerous one at that. Turning to the Buddha without as our focus can help diminish that ingrained cultural egoism and lead to a more balanced awakening that locates the Buddha not inside, but in all.

When *shunyata* is realized, we see that our fundamental nature is not one of inner buddhaness, but of an existence which is completely relational in nature. Thus observing the relations that underlie our practice is a powerful tool for waking up to who and how we really are, one which "de-centers" the inherent pitfall of self-orientation contained in the quest for inner buddhas.

—Jeff Wilson,
Buddhism of the Heart

35

You know that all beings that are born will die. All beings wish for happiness and wish to avoid suffering. Can you live viewing all beings as friends who share birth, old age, sickness, and death? Recite and contemplate this one sentence: "All beings are my friends who share birth, aging, sickness, and death." With every person or animal that you see, with each sound you hear, each sensation you feel, each taste you experience, quietly consider all the beings involved and reflect: "You are my friend who shares birth, old age, sickness, and death." With each contact—be they bugs, neighbors, children, birds, be it the sound of people passing on the road, the smell of cooked meat, the awareness of passengers in airplanes overhead, memories of people, portraits in the newspaper—contemplate that one sentence: "You are my friend who shares birth, old age, sickness, and death."

—SHAILA CATHERINE,
Wisdom Wide and Deep

36

Try as I might to hit upon some strategy that is guaranteed to always work, it never happens. How do I get myself to remember to let go of everything *all the time*?

What about all the times I forget to do that?

———

As Lao-tzu once said, "Thinking only goes as far as that which it can understand."

———

All language is one language.

All sound is one sound.

—JANE DOBISZ,
One Hundred Days of Solitude

37

Perfection and change aren't opposites; they turn out to be synonyms.

—

One paradox into which many practitioners fall is that having affirmed the emptiness or impermanence of all conditions, including inner ones, they then valorize "enlightenment" precisely as an unchanging, permanent inner state they hope one day to achieve.

—

In the end, what we may need to be most free of, what keeps us most in bondage, is the very fantasy of absolute freedom itself.

—

Our practice is a dialectic between self-discovery (what no one can do for us) and self-forgetting (a forsaking of will and a surrender into a life and practice that is not of our creation).

—Barry Magid,
Nothing Is Hidden

38

Sometimes we assume it is through the inner commentary that we know the world. Actually, that inner speech does not know the world at all. It is the inner speech that spins the delusions that cause suffering. Inner speech causes us to be angry with our enemies and to form dangerous attachments to our loved ones. Inner speech causes all of life's problems. It constructs fear and guilt, anxiety and depression. It builds these illusions as deftly as the skillful actor manipulates the audience to create terror or tears. So if you seek truth, you should value silent awareness and, when meditating, consider it more important than any thought.

It is the high value that one gives to one's own thoughts that is the main obstacle to silent awareness. Wisely removing the importance that one gives to thinking, and realizing the greater accuracy of silent awareness, opens the door to inner silence.

—AJAHN BRAHM,
Mindfulness, Bliss, and Beyond

39

We must die to each moment and allow life to express itself through us. Our lives may not turn out the way in which the ego has imagined, but when we surrender to the truth of what is, we will find freedom beyond measure as surely as the river finds its way to the sea. When we move beyond the dualistic world, there is a rebirth into the deathless. We finally come home to a place that we have really never left.

—MATTHEW FLICKSTEIN,
The Meditator's Atlas

40

Thus, we can say that to truly love and follow the Buddha is also to love and care for the world, which is also to love and care for other living beings. And the reverse is equally true: to really care for others is at the same time devotion to the Buddha.

—GENE REEVES,
The Stories of the Lotus Sutra

41

Karma represents the sum total of cause and effect in our lives; the causes that have made us who we are, the effects we create moment after moment in response to those causes.

———

At the most basic level of daily practice, we participate in *ritual*, literally entering into the forms and actions of our ancestors. Ritual is an opportunity to surrender our individual likes and dislikes, our personal opinions about how and why something is done. At the symbolic and psychological level, surrender stands in for the traditional monastic practice of home-leaving. We leave the presumed safety of our self-centeredness and surrender our own point of view to that of the tradition, and to the Dharma.

———

We will be unable to participate in the oneness of all existence if we are unable to experience the totality of our own selves. Splitting off and disowning aspects of our self, we create a damaged, divided world in which we strive after an elusive transcendental wholeness.

—BARRY MAGID, *Nothing Is Hidden*

42

We do not need to take on the burden of adopting traditional language and culture to practice, but it is very important to understand or appreciate as much as possible about the linguistic, cultural, and historical threads that support traditional Buddhist practice to have a full and robust appreciation for its purpose. Such a contextualized understanding allows us to appreciate the deep meaning of Buddhism as a path of liberation and keeps us from reducing it to the fulfillment of our perceived psychological needs.

—HARVEY ARONSON
IN *Buddhism and Psychotherapy Across Cultures*

43

There is evidence that people who view their work as a calling obtain more satisfaction from it then those who work primarily for money or for advancement. The practice of vow is similar. When you do your work with a sense of satisfaction in being helpful to others, in making a difference, paradoxically, you will be the first one to benefit.

—THOMAS BIEN,
Mindful Therapy

44

Mahamudra meditation is a direct experience of the mind as it is and not an attempt to alter or create it. The mind's nature does not have to be changed, and, actually, the true nature cannot be created or recreated. Nevertheless, this instruction does not mean that we should allow ourselves to be distracted by thoughts or disturbing emotions. The freedom from alteration does not mean allowing ourselves to be drawn away; it means freedom from the conceptually directed meditation of attempting to achieve a certain state. For example, while meditating we may think, "I must experience this emptiness. The mind is brilliant lucidity and I must perceive this lucidity." The primary intent of the instruction is to be free from this discursiveness.

—KHENCHEN THRANGU RINPOCHE,
A Song for the King

45

When we throw ourselves into zazen, into this very life, we enter the gate of joyful ease and the Way is complete in all the ten directions. *Right here* is the truth-happening place, and the shoes that are already on our feet fit so nicely. At such a time, enlightenment is fully intimate with suffering. This or that pain or complaint co-create this moment along with the rattle of the far-off crow.

The second most important thing, friend, is not to worry about *you*. Don't worry about you if you are just taking up Zen or if you have practiced wholeheartedly for many long years, through many long retreats, with or without the results you desire. Forget attainment or nonattainment and just burn completely in zazen and in each activity day and night.

The most important thing is the strength of the Way-Seeking Heart.

—DOSHO PORT,
Keep Me in Your Heart a While

46

The pull toward spiritual practice always comes, on some level, from a sense that universal love is natural, that it can should be lived and expressed.

—LES KAYE,
Joyously Through the Days

47

Doubt can be the most insidious and damaging hindrance if it is left unchecked. Doubt does not relate to a dogma, doctrine, technique, or belief system. It is the more deep-seated doubt in your own ability: a doubt about whether you can make progress in training your mind and achieving more of your innate potential. In contemporary society many people are hampered with feelings of low self-worth; it almost seems to be a disease of modernity. The best antidote to the hindrance of doubt is to find people, books, ideas, and teachers that inspire you to think big about yourself, and then to follow up these sources of inspiration.

—

You may need to find a wise teacher or mentor, and this may require a long and arduous search. Sometimes we have to reach out humbly to friends we have neglected, or take the risk of trying to extend a friendship into a deeper level of openness and intimacy.

—BOB SHARPLES,
Meditation and Relaxation in Plain English

48

The Buddha said that doubt is the most challenging of the hindrances because it is self-generated and therefore seems so rational.

—LAURA S.,
12 Steps on the Buddha's Path

49

I don't necessarily have to be slapped in the face in order to wake up; I need only to be momentarily plucked up out of whatever comforting narrative I've designed for myself and dropped back into the world as it is. Encountering a grinning child with freckles and a missing baby tooth will easily do the trick, or a woman running in the park with her pigtails flopping from side to side, or a loosened leaf drifting down from overhead, or a man in a parking lot talking heatedly into a cell phone, or the call of sandhill cranes passing overhead in the dark of night. When the world awakens me like this, all sorts of options appear that I had no idea were present before.

—LIN JENSEN,
Together Under One Roof

50

Why be unhappy about something
if it can be remedied?
And what is the use of being unhappy about something
if it cannot be remedied?

—SHANTIDEVA
IN *Buddhist Psychology*

51

All we have is now—and in this now, each other.

—ROBERT LANGAN,
Minding What Matters

52

Religion at its best encourages us to understand and subvert the destructive dualism between self and other, and between collective self and collective other. This kind of selfless universalism—or, better, nondiscrimination that does not place *us* over *them*—provides the basis for Buddhist social action.

———

The early Buddhist sutras usually define enlightenment in negative terms, as the *end* of craving and dukkha. In a similar fashion, we can envision the solution to social dukkha as a society that does not institutionalize greed, ill will, or delusion. In their place, what might be called a dharmic society would have institutions encouraging their positive counterparts: generosity and compassion, grounded in a wisdom that recognizes our interconnectedness.

—DAVID LOY
IN *Mindful Politics*

53

We appear in the world, quite real, but without finite edges. Turns out we are not complete and autonomous; rather we bleed out into the universe, into openness. Or perhaps it's better to say we arise out of, are sustained by, and return to that openness, that boundlessness. A traditional Zen word for this aspect of what we are is "empty." You might think of this *Empty* as our family name. You and I, and flies and lice, and stars and planets, and heat and cold—those are our personal names. But we also all belong to the great Empty family.

—JAMES ISHMAEL FORD,
If You're Lucky, Your Heart Will Break

54

The very first opportunity for mindfulness occurs as you transition from sleep into wakefulness. If you bring mindful attention to the process of waking, you may start to find that the quality and texture of your day differs from simply moving automatically through your morning routine.

The objective in waking mindfully is paying attention, deeply, regardless of whether your immediate experience is marked by calm or chaos.

—DEBORAH SCHOEBERLEIN,
Mindful Teaching and Teaching Mindfulness

55

Four "Commonplace" Truths

1. No situation is impossible to change.
2. A communal vision, outstanding strategy, and sustained effort can bring forth positive changes.
3. Everyone can help make a difference.
4. No one is free of responsibility.

—KAZUAKI TANAHASHI
IN *Mindful Politics*

56

This practice is beautifully summed up in one of the Buddha's shortest teachings. He simply said, "In seeing, let there be only what is seen; in hearing, let there be only what is heard; in sensing, let there be only what is sensed; in cognizing, let there be only what is cognized." The point is to be fully aware of our experience, without adding interpretation or commentary, without getting lost in it, clinging to it, or pushing it away. This means simply being with what is happening right now, being fully present to the moment. It means surrendered acceptance of "what is," whether agreeable to us or not, without reactive emotions. It does not mean passivity in the face of evil or when action is called for, but only that we act out of the needs of the situation and not from our own reactivity.

—MARY JO MEADOW,
Christian Insight Meditation

57

Desire cannot give you real satisfaction, but it's difficult to give up hoping that it might be able to—and trying just once more.

—Urgyen Sangharakshita,
The Essential Sangharakshita

58

Sometimes people imagine compassion as being passive and kind of wimpy, but genuine compassion is fearlessness. The other side of Avalokiteshvara, the bodhisattva of compassion, is the fierce-looking Tibetan deity Mahakala, with flames coming from his head. Those are the flames of wisdom, while Mahakala's heart is compassion itself. There are times when compassion means standing in strength, but it's not ego power and it's not based on anger. Compassion is actually the most fearless emotion in the world.

—TENZIN PALMO
IN *The Best of Inquiring Mind*

59

Mindfulness practice helps us to see all the productions of the self, layer by layer—and it helps us to not identify with any of the selves as the "final" word on who we are. Practice helps us to see the ephemeral, changing nature of self and to appreciate the process of change itself.

—ARNIE KOZAK,
Wild Chickens and Petty Tyrants

60

When a single flower blooms, it is spring throughout the world.

———

Right here within the mud of our desires, we find the flower of enlightenment blooming. Right within our delusions, amid our impurities, we find our heart opening and our mind awakening.

—SHODO HARADA,
Moon by the Window

61

Feeling certain, of course, is no guarantee of being right.

—

We must center our practice not on coming up with new answers to our questions, but on bringing to light the old answers we carry around inside us and which form the hard shell of Self that stands between us and Life.

—BARRY MAGID,
Ending the Pursuit of Happiness

62

By accepting as a fundamental axiom that suffering is present as an inescapable component of the human condition, Buddhists make way for a higher-level framing and resolution of the problem. They aspire to a state of well-being that can encompass pain, rather than one that depends on the unrealistic suppression or avoidance of pain. Similarly, they strive to experience pleasure without attachment to or dependence upon its perpetuation. This is done by cultivating *equanimity*, which is a way of being present with pleasure without attachment and of being present with pain without resistance. Equanimity embraces both pleasure and pain, and by doing so can bear them both without suffering.

—ANDREW OLENDZKI,
Unlimiting Mind

63

Ill will toward yourself is something that you should watch out for in meditation. It may be the main hindrance that is stopping you from getting deep into meditation.

—

To sum up, ill will is a hindrance, and you overcome that hindrance by compassion to all others, forgiveness toward yourself, loving-kindness toward the meditation object, goodwill toward the meditation, and friendship toward the breath. You can have loving-kindness toward silence and the present moment too. When you care for these friends who reside in the mind, you overcome any aversion toward them as meditation objects.

—AJAHN BRAHM,
Mindfulness, Bliss, and Beyond

64

What is compassion? Compassion involves a feeling of closeness to others, a respect and affection that is not based on others' attitude toward us. We tend to feel affection for people who are important to us. That kind of close feeling does not extend to our enemies—those who think ill of us. Genuine compassion, on the other hand, sees that others, just like us, want a happy and successful life and do not want to suffer. That kind of feeling and concern can be extended to friend and enemy alike, regardless of their feelings toward us. That's genuine compassion.

—THE DALAI LAMA,
The Middle Way

65

The molting of birds can be either sudden or gradual. These variants of the molt seem to me particularly analogous and expressive of what Zen calls "awakening"—the self losing itself in order to realize itself, the self settling into itself, awakening to what it truly is. It's an awakening that might come with the startling suddenness of brilliant new feathers or arrive in increments, one feather at a time, in a transformation so subtle as to be nearly indiscernible until complete.

Awakening may result in radically altered plumage but the crucial insight, the actual enlightenment, is not so much about getting new feathers as it is about being stripped of the old. Awakening is within the interim between molts when what you were before has passed away and what you are to become is not yet realized. Awakening arises in times of vulnerability and awkwardness between "before" and "after," where prior identities are cancelled and anything is possible and nothing certain. It is in that place of no-place and in that "person" of no particularity that you come closest to the source of all feathers and to the act of feathering itself.

—LIN JENSEN,
Together Under One Roof

66

Receiving benefits that I can't in good conscience claim to deserve, I am motivated to try to make sure that others receive such gifts as well. And I remember that while political, social, and economic benefits are crucial, even the drawing of breath from moment to moment is a gift provided by the universe through no action of my own.

—JEFF WILSON,
Buddhism of the Heart

67

If you think, "This is it,"

that will plant the seed of attachment to an object.

If the seedling of conceit appears,

it will grow into the tree of samsara.

In brief, rest the mind without thinking, "This is it!"

Rest the mind without thinking, "This isn't it!"

The mind's thoughts of "is" and the mind's thoughts
   of "isn't"

are two mutually dependent fixations.

If there is absolutely no "is" at all,

then there will be absolutely no "isn't" at all.

—LAMA SHANG

IN *Mahamudra and Related Instructions*

68

When we hear about or think about the mind, our mind is labeling a particular phenomenon "mind," and we then believe that there is a mind. There is no unlabeled mind. Mind is just a concept.

—

The concept of true existence is completely unnecessary.

—LAMA ZOPA RINPOCHE,
How to Be Happy

69

When cultivating a compassionate mental state, sometimes I look for words that address the source of the suffering, anguish, or stress. The source is, of course, what the second noble truth points to: the desire for things to be other than they are. I might silently say, "It's so hard to want so badly not to be sick." Other times, I look for words that simply open my heart to the suffering, such as, "My poor body, working so hard to feel better." Whatever words I choose, I often stroke one arm with the hand of the other. This has brought me to tears many times, but tears of compassion are healing tears.

—TONI BERNHARD,
How to Be Sick

70

If I do not struggle with the greed inside myself, it is quite likely that, once in power, I too will be inclined to take advantage of the situation to serve my own interests. If I do not acknowledge the ill will in my own heart, I am likely to project my anger onto those who obstruct my purposes. If unaware that my own sense of duality is a dangerous delusion, I will understand the problem of social change as the need for me to dominate the sociopolitical order. Add a conviction of my good intentions, along with my superior understanding of the situation, and one has a recipe for social as well as personal disaster.

—DAVID LOY
IN *Mindful Politics*

71

We can extend Wise Speech to include listening. Giving attention is one of the purest expressions of love we can make. When we give each other the gift of listening with our whole hearts, separation dissolves and hurt is healed.

—ARINNA WEISMAN AND JEAN SMITH,
The Beginner's Guide to Insight Meditation

72

I took my first steps toward experiencing happiness when I learned an important Dharma lesson about suffering: none of the sources of suffering are personal. They don't happen just to *me*; they happen to everyone. The more deeply I understood the universality of suffering, the easier it was for me to not cling to and identify with the sources of my suffering or to the suffering itself by telling myself stories about it.

—LAURA S.,
12 Steps on the Buddha's Path

73

To be fully and completely alive, fully and completely human, is goal enough. There is no other sort of completeness or perfection to attain. The plum tree in my backyard can only express its plum tree–ness. No other kind of perfection is available or needed. A flower is only itself. It does not have to strain and struggle to be a flower, but lets its flowerness unfold of itself.

You may ask, "Who am I to do this work?" and I might respond, "Who are you *not* to do this?"

—THOMAS BIEN,
Mindful Therapy

74

You follow desire and you are not satisfied. Again you follow desire, and again you are not satisfied. Again you try, and again you are not satisfied.

—

Desire is like honey on a razor's edge: it looks like pleasure but offers only pain.

—

You follow desire with the aim of getting satisfaction. Your aim is worthwhile and you are right to wish to obtain it—but the method is wrong and results only in dissatisfaction.

—LAMA ZOPA RINPOCHE,
How to Be Happy

75

If one can learn to be nonattached to a particular notion of oneself, and become able to open to new iterations of oneself, new possibilities of becoming a different person in various ways, then the lack of rigid self-identification is more a blessing than a curse. The person who was traumatized in the past need not be the same person who may be free of the impact of that trauma in the future. There may well be a person here now who feels unworthy or unloved, incapable of happiness, but that same person may be nowhere to be seen even a few moments from now. The person deeply caught in cycles of addiction today may be just a character in a story told by a healthier person tomorrow.

The profound plasticity of self, if it can be seen for oneself in the moment-to-moment flow of experience, can be a spectacularly liberating experience.

—ANDREW OLENDZKI,
Unlimiting Mind

76

Mere suffering exists, no sufferer is found;
The deeds are, but no doer of the deeds is there;
Nibbana is, but not the person that enters it;
The path is, but no traveler on it is seen.

—*Visuddhimagga* 16:90,
IN *Mindfulness, Bliss, and Beyond*

77

The first thing I want to do is set aside the word *enlightenment*, which is obscured behind a cloud of mythology and projection. Instead, I'll speak of awakening, which is a journey that unfolds over a lifetime, in the way particular to each person who makes it. Awakening is the process of opening the heart and clarifying the mind that is made real in a person's life. It isn't a destination; it's the path each of us is already walking, and it's unfolding in big and small ways all the time.

—JOAN SUTHERLAND
IN *The Book of Mu*

78

After most moments of enlightenment, doubt is usually just around the corner.

—JANET JIRYU ABELS,
Making Zen Your Own

79

A lie is you deceiving yourself. The one who deceives and the one who is deceived is you.

—DAEHAENG SUNIM,
No River to Cross

80

"Oh, I get it!" said Monkey. "Mind-*full*, like your mind is full of the present, full of right now. That's definitely how I want to be!"

—LAUREN ALDERFER,
Mindful Monkey, Happy Panda

81

A central tenet of meditation practice is that motivation is everything.

—

The paradox of meditation is that it is both simple and difficult. It is a simple thing to do yet it requires discipline and effort to do it regularly. Clarity of motivation may be the thing that will encourage you to put that regular time aside each day.

—BOB SHARPLES,
Meditation and Relaxation in Plain English

82

Transcendence, in fact, is ordinary. Feelings and thoughts and actions make up the world. Ordinarily, we look out for one another without much thought. To be more responsible for feelings and thoughts and actions, to assess their harm and benefit, is to live more with others in mind. By my actions, including the action of turning my attention to this over that, I shape myself, and I shape the world. My actions have consequences attention foresees and consequences that transcend the foreseeable. I shape the world; I dwell in the world given shape by the actions of others.

—ROBERT LANGAN,
Minding What Matters

83

Meditation has to do with how we direct our consciousness. Wisdom has to do with the truths that arise out of our deep knowing of intimate connectedness. And wise conduct, or morality, has to do with living in harmony with the world we encounter, a life in which we cause ourselves and others ever less and less harm.

———

Awakening is not a thing, nor is it a thought, nor is it even an *experience*—rather it is noticing what is: the first time perhaps dramatically, but then over, and over, and over, and deeper and deeper and deeper, in each undramatic moment of our lives.

Awakening is not something "out there" or "down the line." It happens in a mysterious, curious, wondrous moment; completely beyond any planning or hope. This is an important teaching: it tells us the possibility for awakening, for freedom, is always available to us right here, right now. Moreover, we don't *earn* it. This awakening arose within the mind of an ordinary woodcutter, not a Buddha or a saint, or even a master meditator. This is wondrous good news— and I really want to underscore this point—for it shows that awakening is something such ordinary folk as you and I can achieve, just as we are.

—JAMES ISHMAEL FORD,
Zen Master WHO?

84

When circumstances snatched my prior realities away from me, it was useless to try and get them back or substitute some contrivance in their stead. All I could do was bow to the situation. And when I did, I freed myself from my part in the drama, watching it unfold as if it had nothing to do with me.

—LIN JENSEN,
Together Under One Roof

85

I don't think I ever found and lost a great poem on the cushion…. Would it were so easy.

—JANE HIRSHFIELD
IN *Women Practicing Buddhism*

86

Reflect on what you plan to say before you say it. Why are you speaking? Are you avoiding the extremes of brutal honesty and inauthenticity?

—ANYEN RINPOCHE,
Momentary Buddhahood

87

The first Ennobling Truth is usually (and poorly) translated as "Life is suffering." This is the Buddha's diagnosis of the human situation. *Suffering* is the key word here, but it is much more nuanced than the English word *suffering*. The Sanskrit word is *duhkha*. Etymologically, *kha* means the hub of a wheel; and the prefix *duh* is something like the English prefix "mis," as when we say something is "mis-placed" or "mis-taken." The word *duhkha*, therefore, points to a situation wherein the hub of a wheel is not properly centered; it is dislocated, and so the wheel is not functioning the way it should. The first Ennobling Truth is a basic recognition that all is not well with the way we are living our human lives. Another translation of *duhkha* is *dis-ease*—with the emphasis on the hyphen.

—RUBEN L. F. HABITO,
Healing Breath

88

It is not understood by those who understand It.
It is understood by those who understand It not.

—*Kena Upanishad*
IN *The World Is Made of Stories*

Do I contradict myself?
Very well, then I contradict myself,
I am large, I contain multitudes.

—WALT WHITMAN
IN *The World Is Made of Stories*

89

The most profound and effective way to overcome sloth and torpor is to stop fighting your mind. Stop trying to change things and instead let things be. Make peace not war with sloth and torpor.

—AJAHN BRAHM,
Mindfulness, Bliss, and Beyond

90

The greatest freedom is freedom from the illusion that we are not already free.

———

Nothing exists—not even nothing.

—MATTHEW FLICKSTEIN,
The Meditator's Atlas

91

Letting go of our own preconceptions and ambitions, seeing more of the totality of the situation, we can look with respect, understanding, and evenness at other people and what they are going through. Without reacting, we provide psychological room for them to see themselves, as if in a mirror. More than that, we can abide patiently, looking for the moment when genuine communication becomes possible and we can address the situation in a precise and effective way.

—REGINALD A. RAY
IN *Mindful Politics*

92

Every instance when we create separation through anger, blame, or building ourselves up at others' expense is *selfing*. All human beings seem to need to go through selfing early in life to establish a sense of identity and to develop emotionally, but many people concretize the *I-me-my* and never seem to join the human race or recognize the interrelationship of all beings.

———

When we are able to see the impermanence of the feelings that we get so wrapped up in, it becomes increasingly easy to let go of them—"to lose interest in selfish things." We can see that just as we can get caught up in selfing, so do those around us. We learn to remember that just as our selfing is impermanent, so is theirs. In this way, we can allow ourselves to be truly in and with the present moment and can open to others without the dualistic judgmentalism we usually use to drive wedges between us, and we can take genuine interest in them.

—LAURA S.,
12 Steps on the Buddha's Path

93

We mustn't confuse spiritual aspiration with a striving for some kind of insipid, limp goodness.

—

Mindfulness is a way of facing the truth.

—THOMAS BIEN,
Mindful Therapy

94

When we encounter fear and simply know it as it is, fear is transmuted. The experience is transformed into one of strength and confidence.

—AJAHN SUNDARA
IN *The Best of Inquiring Mind*

95

Environmentalists talk about "cleaning up after the elephant"—the endless task of cleaning up industrial contamination—and how a far more effective strategy is to avoid fouling up the environment in the first place. Likewise, mindfulness of breathing can be used to prevent the contamination of our inner environment. It helps us tether the elephant of the mind and avoid the imbalances that so frequently come with modern living.

The healing of the body-mind has another significant parallel with environmentalist ideas. When a stream is polluted, one may try to add antidotes to the toxins in the water, hoping such additives will neutralize the damage. But the more straightforward and sensible approach is simply to stop the flow of contamination into the stream. When this is done, over time the flow of the water through soil, stones, and vegetation can purify the stream completely.

—B. ALAN WALLACE,
The Attention Revolution

96

For monastic practitioners, life structured by rules and schedules provides moment-by-moment opportunities to let go of preferences and manifest no-self, but an over-emphasis on no-self can lead to spiritual bypassing, in which personal feelings and impulses remain repressed and unintegrated. The difficulty arises when the relinquishing of self-clinging thoughts on the meditation cushion, or the abandoning of preferences, is mistakenly translated as *having no feelings* when interacting with other people. Far too often, monastic Zen students may confuse detachment or emotional distancing and repression for noticing with a nonattached mind. Staying connected to loved ones not only does not interfere with their awakening, but it provides relationship skills in working with their sanghas.

—GRACE SCHIRESON,
Zen Women

97

This Dharma is indescribable.
Words must fall silent.
Among other kinds of living beings,
None can understand it,
Except the bodhisattvas,
Whose faith is strong and firm.

Even disciples of the Buddha
Who have made offerings to buddhas,
Gotten rid of all their faults,
And now live in their final incarnation,
Even such people as these,
Don't have this much power.

Even a world
Full of men like Shariputra,
Using all of their mental powers together
Could not fathom Buddha-wisdom.

Indeed, if all the worlds in the ten directions
Were full of people like Shariputra
Or any other disciples,

Filling all the worlds,
Using all of their mental powers together,
None of these people could fathom it.

—BUDDHA
IN *The Lotus Sutra*

98

If you care to notice, the morning star shines everywhere—in the eye of a child, in the faces of sunflowers tracking their namesake across the sky, in the sudden flash of trout feeding in the whitewater rapids, in the haunting mimicry of a mockingbird, in your own reflection in the bathroom mirror, and, yes, in the tracings of earthworms on fallen leaves. Once seen in its own right, the morning star binds all life together in one inseparable body. At whatever time and place you recognize its rising will be the very time and place of the Buddha's enlightenment.

—LIN JENSEN,
Deep Down Things

99

With each small venture into the unknown, I am rewarded with a new feeling: "I can do it!" It's very empowering. When you let go of your small self and bow to your true self, it's like saying to the world, "Please teach me. I am open to learning. I want to be with you."

Who would have ever thought that bowing, of all things, could teach you courage?

———

don't know
don't know
always and everywhere
only don't know

—JANE DOBISZ,
One Hundred Days of Solitude

100

A real spiritual practice plays rough with the ego.

—

The Way is vast and endlessly forgiving. It is also harsh, demanding everything from us. But this "everything" is not about how much time you choose to put on the pillow.

—JAMES ISHMAEL FORD,
If You're Lucky, Your Heart Will Break

101

In short, that entity we naïvely take to be a person is actually a swirling confluence of mental and physical factors all arising together in concert, mutually conditioning one another for an indescribably brief moment of interaction, and then passing away together to make room for the next moment's configuration.

—ANDREW OLENDZKI,
Unlimiting Mind

102

Ordinary love is biased and mixed with attachment. Like other afflicted emotions, attachment is based not on reality but on mental projection. It exaggerates reality. In reality there may be some good there, but attachment views it as one hundred percent beautiful or good. Compassion gets much closer to reality. There is a vast difference.

—THE DALAI LAMA,
The Middle Way

103

In brief, to think that things "are" is the root of attachment
   to everything.
From the root of attachment all samsara develops.

—LAMA SHANG
IN *Mahamudra and Related Instructions*

104

Reality is the sameness of whatever arises, abides, and subsides. Or to say it another way, neither sense impressions nor thoughts—nothing whatsoever—stirs from the spaciousness of pure being as they entwine in the matrix of the three dimensions of spontaneous creativity. The matrix is always still and silent. The media of body, speech, and mind partake of that stasis.

There is no movement in pure mind, no process, no development, no flow, no continuum, no transformation, no change of any kind. Each moment is complete and perfect in itself and always released at its inception.

Reflexive release of thought and sense impression is maintained without any trace of duality by instantaneous potentiation of emotionally charged experience.

—KEITH DOWMAN,
Natural Perfection

105

What if all happiness anywhere is your happiness?

—LAMA ZOPA RINPOCHE,
How to Be Happy

106

Can we actually be present with *this* body and mind as it is, not our ideas of who we are, but actually be present with the physical sensation and the swirling thoughts that are happening on our cushion, right now? Without trying to get anything from it, and also not trying to get rid of it, do not hold back at all. Do not hold back from just fully enjoying or engaging this present experience, whether you feel good, bad, or indifferent about it. This is the heart of zazen practice.

—

When we really pay attention to this body and mind, we see how deeply we are connected with everyone and everything, right as we sit here now.

—

Just sit and be with this as this. Be with that just as that. Do not hold back from yourself.

—Taigen Dan Leighton,
Zen Questions

107

The awareness of feeling that we are in hell—that our life is not flowing—is as much an opportunity as it is a problem. The pain of the feeling is a wake-up call, a chance to explore our life, to understand our self, and to see the reason behind our suffering. However, if we deny the feeling, if we are unwilling to do the work of spiritual practice, we will find that there is "no work" and will remain in hell. Acknowledging our hell-bound feeling is the starting point for understanding that we are caught up in attachments and preconceived ideas.

—LES KAYE,
Joyously Through the Days

108

The Buddha had a great deal to say about communication—about the importance of truthful, kindly, meaningful, and harmonious speech, and about the necessity to pay attention to one's relationships in general, making sure that one is relating in ways that accord with one's Buddhist principles.

The reasons for this are quite obvious. To be human is to be related to other human beings. We cannot live our lives in isolation; whatever efforts we make to develop as individuals are continually tested in the fires of our relationships with other people. However calm, kind, and wise we may feel in the privacy of our own hearts or shrine-rooms, the true test of how fully we have developed these qualities comes when we are faced with the realities of life as represented by the challenges offered by "other people."

—

The real significance of the deep individual-to-individual contact that Going for Refuge to the Sangha involves lies in a simple psychological fact: we get to know ourselves best in relation to other people.

—URGYEN SANGHARAKSHITA,
The Essential Sangharakshita

109

When I first explored setting intentions, I immediately set lofty goals such as to "stay patient with everyone, all day" and to "refrain from feeling angry about anything ever." Perhaps unsurprisingly, I forgot most of these lofty first intentions almost as quickly as I made them. When I did manage to remember them in the midst of a trying day, my objectives appeared so unrealistic as to be unreachable and, therefore, irrelevant to me in any given moment. Eventually, I learned to change my approach, setting more modest and achievable intentions—and, as a result, meeting my goals more and more often. Much later, as my skills and confidence grew, I was able to increase the scope of my aspiration in reasonable increments.

Behavioral intentions provide a constructive starting point because they are often the most obvious objectives. For example, after greeting the day, you could set the intention to eat breakfast slowly and carefully chew at least *some* bites, *on this particular morning.*

—DEBORAH SCHOEBERLEIN,
Mindful Teaching and Teaching Mindfulness

IIO

In Buddhism, *regret* is not guilt. Guilt is an ego-driven emotion and as such is always nonvirtuous, but regret can be either virtuous or nonvirtuous. It is virtuous when we have a strong regret for the negative things we have done in the past, consciously or unconsciously, acting under the power of attachment, anger, jealousy, and the like. To see that the harmful actions of body, speech, and mind are negative and should be avoided, and to feel regret that we have done them, is positive in that it leaves a definite imprint on our mindstreams that will help us to avoid such actions in the future.

—GESHE TASHI TSERING,
Buddhist Psychology

III

The bigger picture is that there's a kind of perfection in the universe that includes all the happiness and suffering, all the pain and pleasure, all our successes and failures, and even our death. At a certain point, we begin to experience everything that goes on as part of a perfect, seamless, unimpeachable unfolding of things as they are.

When you realize this about life, it helps you to relax; it helps you let go of your "me" all that more readily. You do engage, but less neurotically, less invested in the success and failure of what you do. To relax in this way doesn't mean that you stop trying. You might even try harder and be willing to take more risks.

—REGINALD A. RAY
IN *Mindful Politics*

112

If you are regularly vexed by certain situations or people, you may like to mentally assign these as periods in which to ensure your mindfulness is switched to high alert. If you're usually driven crazy by driving to work, dealing with a particular client/subcontractor, or another everyday situation perhaps involving a family member, you may like to assign these situations, right now, as times during which you have a tailor-made opportunity to practice the perfection of patience. From now on, think of these as research opportunities for a new cognitive experiment, one in which you will attempt to identify and replace a habitual negative reaction with an alternative that is immeasurably more positive.

—DAVID MICHIE,
Enlightenment To Go

113

It's common to fear exposing our faults, so we may wear a mask of false selflessness. But what we need to do is develop trust in the embracing ocean of the Dharma. Hiding oneself is ultimately a crisis of faith, an action that says "I don't really trust that things will be alright unless I pretend to be something I'm not." If we have confidence that the process of Dharma will work out our liberation naturally, we can let go of the mask and let ourselves be worn down through the working of Other Power, which is the active expression of Dharma.

—JEFF WILSON,
Buddhism of the Heart

114

The natural integrity of consciousness is, I think, very good news for all of us—both as individuals and collectively. What it means for personal development is that one naturally evolves in morality as one progresses in understanding. As we practice meditation and slowly learn to see ourselves more clearly, we also gain an intuitive ability to discern the difference in experience between a wholesome or unwholesome thought, or word, or deed. Advances in integrity, meditation, and understanding all proceed together in a way that gradually guides our path away from suffering and toward the extinguishing of afflictive emotions.

—ANDREW OLENDZKI,
Unlimiting Mind

115

The world of dew
Is the world of dew.
And yet, and yet...

—Issa

in *Heaven and Earth Are Flowers*

116

In the time of the Buddha, a young mother's son became very ill and died. She was overcome with grief. She went to the Buddha and asked him to bring her son back to life. He said he would help her, but first she had to bring him a mustard seed from the home of a person who had never known anyone who died. She had hope and set off. She searched through many villages and for a long time no one could give her what she thought she needed. Finally she found what the Buddha had really sent her to find, the truth that he was trying to teach her: the truth that she wasn't alone in her suffering, that death comes to everyone. She brought her son's body to the charnel ground and let him go. She returned to the Buddha and told him that she had found the real cure that he was offering her and asked him to be her teacher.

—KATHLEEN WILLIS MORTON,
The Blue Poppy and the Mustard Seed

117

Just as perceived images fade away
While one gazes at the expanse of space,
So do discriminating thoughts
When one watches the mind,
And illumination is attained.
For example, mist and clouds loom over a wide space,
And neither proceed toward any destination nor do
    they dwell anywhere.
Likewise, although discriminating thoughts arise from
    the mind,
These thought waves dissolve themselves when the
    meditator perceives the mind.

—TILOPA
IN *Mahamudra—The Moonlight*

118

There is no such thing called "ultimate truth" outside your everyday life. You may go to meditation classes to seek enlightenment; but if you neglect to look for it in front of your nose, you will never find it, no matter how many weeks of seclusion you faithfully attend.

—

What is philosophical in Buddhism is no more than a preliminary step toward what is practical in it.

—NYOGEN SENZAKI,
Eloquent Silence

119

As our attachment to people and things lessens, this doesn't mean we won't like them anymore and will want to get rid of them. On the contrary, we can continue to enjoy them, but without attachment; this actually means we will cherish them even more.

—KATHLEEN MCDONALD,
Awakening the Kind Heart

120

When giving instruction for full bows, Katagiri Roshi taught us with a twinkle in his eyes to raise our hands gently because in this part of the bow we were uplifting the Buddha. "Do not flip hands up quickly or Buddha will fly over you," he joked.

—DOSHO PORT,
Keep Me in Your Heart a While

121

Where there is nothing there is everything.

—

Seeing with your ears, and hearing with your heart, and understanding with your eyes in the Zen mirrorlike mind, reflecting the universe just as it is—its totality, excluding nothing.

—

All that we do will come from the fact that we allowed ourselves to be used by a creative power.

—ELAINE MACINNES,
The Flowing Bridge

122

I have to be willing to let go of the meanings I attribute to things, however cherished these meanings might seem. I've learned to value the surprises life brings me, even when they pull me loose from familiar moorings and set me adrift. I'd rather float free on an improbable sea of unfamiliar possibilities than seek security in a safe harbor of my own ideas. Besides, I'm less interested now in my ideas about things and more interested in the things themselves—and the things themselves are never what I think they are. They're always only themselves, unexpected and never the same.

—LIN JENSEN,
Together Under One Roof

123

It's we ourselves who really need saving: saving from the idea of saving itself and of ourselves as savers or helpers. We may imagine as Buddhists we should be compassionate, peaceful, kind, helpful—and we should always be devoting all our energies on behalf of others. Well, we don't. Not the way we think we should anyway. But by chanting an idealistic-sounding vow we seem to promise that from now on we'll be compassionate. The problem with this approach to the vow is that it gets us further wedded to the attitude that there is something wrong with us and others that needs fixing.

—BARRY MAGID,
Ending the Pursuit of Happiness

124

If you do not find a way to generate some mindfulness at the beginning of the day it becomes even harder to find the time as the day continues and you get caught up in your inevitably busy life.

One such practice is to find a way to remind yourself to breathe and smile even before you sit up in bed and place a foot on the ground. Remind yourself that this day is a gift, that it is wonderful to be alive, even if the day before you is busy and includes people and tasks you would rather not have to deal with.

Try to find a way to touch the wonderfulness of life even before you get out of bed. Some of the clouds passing through may involve planning and worrying about the day ahead, but at least you can create, alongside such thoughts, the awareness that at its base this is all wonderful.

—THOMAS BIEN,
Mindful Therapy

125

Unknowing is not the blankness of not having a clue, nor is it the delusion of cradling a concept as if it were direct experience. Unknowing is another word for profound willingness; it has infinite depths to show you, and there is always more to un-know.

—SUSAN MURPHY,
Upside-Down Zen

126

If we validate thoughts as truths simply because they originate within our own skull we're going to be in all sorts of trouble.

—ARNIE KOZAK,
Wild Chickens and Petty Tyrants

127

When the veils of spiritual delusion begin to lift, we realize
several things: ultimate truth is outside of time, the labels
we attribute to phenomena are not the things themselves,
all self-images are obstructions to seeing spiritual truth, life
is similar to a waking dream, and the only true meditation
practice is "nonmeditation."

—MATTHEW FLICKSTEIN,
The Meditator's Atlas

128

I meditate because I suffer.

I suffer, therefore I am.

I am, therefore I suffer.

I meditate because there are so many other things to do.

—WES NISKER

IN *The Best of Inquiring Mind*

129

You can practice awareness of emptiness in everyday life by meditating on dependent arising, looking at how everything—self, action, object—is merely imputed. Do this while you are working in the office, talking to people or having meetings, or while you are at home with your family. (But it's probably best not to do this while driving, for instance.) Do it especially when you are having a conversation with someone who is complaining about or criticizing you, which will cause the delusion of anger to arise, and when somebody is praising you, which will cause the delusion of pride to arise. Practice awareness of either dependent arising or emptiness. They're the same; it's one meditation.

—LAMA ZOPA RINPOCHE,
How to Be Happy

130

Do not obscure the mind with the darkness of meditation,
for the mind is primordially pure and luminous,
and meditation will destroy the effortless result.

—LAMA SHANG
IN *Mahamudra and Related Instructions*

131

If we are willing to take an unbiased look, we will find that,
in spite of all our problems and confusion, all our emotional
and psychological ups and downs, there is something basically good about our existence as human beings.

—CHOGYAM TRUNGPA RINPOCHE
IN *Mindful Politics*

132

Zen practice becomes simply "letting things be" as they really are. Every facet of life finds its concrete place in this light. This level of practice could be described as "basking in the miracle of ordinariness." Zen masters describe it wonderfully: "When hungry, eat; when thirsty, take a drink; when sleepy, go to sleep." This is a life in total harmony with one's true nature, an authentic way of living one's life.

Yet, if Zen is just about eating when hungry, drinking when thirsty, sleeping when sleepy, what is the difference between life after awakening and any other life? The answer is *no* difference—and all the difference in the world.

—RUBEN L. F. HABITO,
Healing Breath

133

Desire is often described as the "wanting" mind or the "if only" mind. The time spent in meditation can be absorbed in endless fantasies about what we need to make us happy. Our consumerist and materialistic modern world gives enormous emphasis to feeding this desire. The power of desire can be experienced in many forms and in relation to a wide variety of objects: for example, possessions, relationships, reputation, career, achievement, sexuality, body image. Also there are the "if only" desires that can come up about our meditation practice: if only my mind were not so crazy; if only I had a more comfortable cushion; if only my knees didn't hurt so much; if only I had more time. There is really no end to the "if only" cravings that can arise in meditation. It feels so familiar and comfortable to luxuriate in these constantly arising fantasies.

The best antidote is to train yourself to recognize desire when it comes up while you are meditating, note it, and then simply observe it.

➡

Similarly, the best way to soften the power of aversion patiently is to train yourself to see it when it arises and then observe its presence and energy in your body and mind. If you observe it in this way without reacting, aversion begins to loosen its obsessive grip in the mind, and the energy of aversion starts to dissipate.

—BOB SHARPLES,
Meditation and Relaxation in Plain English

134

Everything in the universe is me, and that is the Pure Land. This is what is meant by seeing the truth in ourselves.

—SHODO HARADA,
Moon by the Window

135

An inconceivably complex interaction of past actions gives rise to each of us, bobbing along awhile for a lifetime, each of us like a bubble in its seemingly separate orb of awareness, each an orbitally curved reflection of an entire world, all the bubbles together like tumbling froth at the breaking crest of a wave in a far-off sea, and that wide sea itself cupped in the spaciousness of a vaulting sky whose darkling depth is without limit. We are buoyed on emptiness.

—ROBERT LANGAN,
Minding What Matters

136

Wise Livelihood includes many aspects of our work life—how we talk to people, how we relate to our work, how we relate to our employers or employees, and how we work with the Precepts within the context of our work.

—ARINNA WEISMAN AND JEAN SMITH,
The Beginner's Guide to Insight Meditation

137

Up in the hall a monk came forth and asked, "When Zen master Danxia burned a wooden buddha for warmth, why did the temple director's eyebrows fall?"

Hengchuan said, "This is precisely what I have doubts about."

The monk said, "Master, you are an enlightened teacher. Why do you too have doubts?"

Hengchuan said, "When no one in the world has doubts, then I will have no doubts."

—

A monk asked, "What was the meaning of Bodhidharma's coming from the west?"

Zhuxian said, "To make you ask."

—FROM *Zen Under the Gun*

138

There are times when the practice suddenly feels dry, the meditation is uninspired, our knees hurt, we've run out of ways to entertain ourselves, there's a fly droning somewhere, and it isn't funny anymore. I learned to walk through these desert places, and even to welcome them. I realized that dry places are way stations where we have exhausted the known and are waiting for the new. There is a patience and kindness with ourselves that develops when we're willing to wait through like this. We can't know what timeframe is appropriate, and it doesn't matter anyhow, our life is always happening right here while we're hoping for something else to happen. If I just sat not wanting very much to happen, little things would open up, and I found that just being given this task of sitting can itself be a form of grace.

—RACHEL MANSFIELD-HOWLETT
IN *The Book of Mu*

139

As the Buddha famously tells a group of villagers, who are confused by the apparent contradictions of various teachings they have heard, "When you know for yourselves that these things are wholesome... these things, when entered upon and undertaken, incline toward welfare and happiness—then having come to them you should stay with them."

—ANDREW OLENDZKI,
Unlimiting Mind

140

"Just sitting" shouldn't be understood as mere quietism; nor is it a way to dwell in states of bliss, suppress our thoughts, or cultivate any kind of blankness. Shikantaza invites us to intimately be within the spaciousness that includes thought, as well as the space outside the thoughts and the very thoughts themselves. We are invited to simply experience the natural expansiveness of our mind and whatever it may reveal—even if what it reveals is an experience of contraction!

—JAMES ISHMAEL FORD,
Zen Master WHO?

141

Meditation is a gentle process of slowing down, allowing thoughts to come and go without attempting to join them or run from them, and permitting oneself a growing place of respite between thoughts that so easily lead to illusory notions of self and others. In such a process there is an increased sense of expansiveness that is not ours alone, but a true web of interbeing.

It is a gentle, inward-looking but outwardly attuned process that is more a *restoration* than a miraculous achievement of something altogether new. It is a kind of homecoming to the good and pure mind of clear seeing.

—PILAR JENNINGS,
Mixing Minds

142

To me, the stoles that we wear in the worship hall (called *kesas*) are our flags of permanent defeat. When you slip the stole over your head and go before Amida Buddha, you are acknowledging that your own power is never enough to get by. You are permanently defeated. Even the stole itself seems to signal this defeat.

That isn't something to celebrate or take pride in. We are only special in the way we have come to realize that we aren't going to reach the goal on our own, that our defeat is permanent, part of our nature, and existed before we even tried. Yet it is by accepting the permanency of our defeat that we become aware of another avenue to the finish line, of the possibility that, odd as it may seem at first, defeat leads to victory when it causes us to relax back into our natural state and simply let Other Power, like the calm but relentless winds and tides, carry us to our destination.

And when surrender has been declared, strangely enough, we are enabled to go forward and live our lives as Buddhists in gratitude, seeking to do good and walk the path—without concerns of winning or losing.

—JEFF WILSON,
Buddhism of the Heart

143

Meditation is lonely as any practice is lonely—no one can make it easier for you, no one can do it for you, and you alone can find the enduring quality within it. But that loneliness gradually reveals a subtle and lovely flavor found nowhere else, and it is oddly familiar and comfortable; it turns out to be an enthralling solitude that teems with life, a nothing-in-particular from which everything emerges fresh. And in solitude you come to know more closely your own strength of unbending intent, which also serves you well in this life. To endure without fuss is an act of mindfulness, which is also a silent gift to others. You can give it away with impunity and never run out.

—Susan Murphy,
Upside-Down Zen

144

"The depth is in the surface."

—WILLIAM MATTHEWS
IN *The Mindful Writer*

Underneath every surface, below every common thought, behind each and every cliché, there is depth, if you will only take the time to look.

It is easy enough to see the surface of things, yet in truth, there are times we can't even accomplish that much. Often, instead of seeing what is there, all we see is what we anticipate will be there, our own attachments and expectations.

—DINTY W. MOORE,
The Mindful Writer

145

Our culture's view of mind.

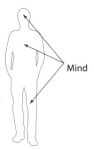

The Buddhist view of mind.

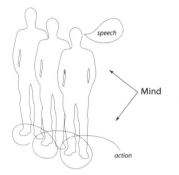

Mind is also embodied in words and action.

The thread of mind extends throughout the whole
of the universe.

—RISHI SATIVIHARI,
Unlearning the Basics

146

Alongside all the other experiences of my life, I made room for fear. I felt a great spaciousness and expansiveness. Soon I became aware that a gentle smile had appeared on my lips as if to say, "Ah, yes. My old friend, fear." And so the seed was sown for a new compassion practice: opening my heart to the full range of emotions that life has in store for me.

—TONI BERNHARD,
How to Be Sick

147

When you are deluded, you are turned by the dharma
  blossom.
When you are awakened, you turn the dharma blossom.
When you leap beyond delusion and awakening,
  the dharma blossom turns the dharma blossom.

—DOGEN
IN *Lotus*

148

If you identify by thinking "It's emptiness,"
or thinking "It is signless and aspirationless,"
thinking "It is unidentifiable," thinking "It is completely pure,"
thinking "It is birthless," thinking "It is unperceivable,"
thinking "It has no nature," thinking "It is without elaboration,"
thinking "It is not an object for analysis by speech or mind,"
thinking "It is uncreated and naturally present," and so on,
however profound these thoughts, our recognition of
    emptiness
will not transcend the conceptualization of an arrogant mind.
Attachment to concepts leads to a fall into inferior states
and a continuous ripening of karma from inferior actions.

—LAMA SHANG
IN *Mahamudra and Related Instructions*

149

Extremely little of each surf session is spent actually standing up on your surfboard on a wave—maybe one percent—so if you're looking to have a good time it's essential to find a way to enjoy paddling out to catch the wave, or at least good-naturedly bear it. And in that way, I thought, surfing is kind of a good metaphor for the rest of life.

The extremely good stuff—chocolate and great sex and weddings and hilarious jokes—fills a minute portion of an adult lifespan.

The rest of life is the paddling: work, paying bills, flossing, getting sick, dying.

I started to entertain the thought that maybe I could start to deal better with that kind of paddling too...

—JAIMAL YOGIS,
Saltwater Buddha

150

If I don't insist on defining impermanence as unsatisfactory, then it's quite natural, indeed unavoidable, to celebrate impermanence. We do it all the time. The sun rises, only to set and then rise again. Water falls from the skies and flows down rivers to the sea where it rises once more to the sky. Just a moment's pause to consider the passing of the seasons is enough to convince anyone that not only is impermanence the source of all possible *joy* in this life but that impermanence is the *movement* of life itself.

—LIN JENSEN,
Together Under One Roof

151

Really, the deal is pretty simple; all one needs to do is just sit down, shut up, and pay attention.

This is the universal solvent of the heart.

Become as wide as the sky.

Let the whole of what is play across the screen of the mind and heart.

Just notice.

—JAMES ISHMAEL FORD,
If You're Lucky, Your Heart Will Break

152

The best way to take care of pain is with a soft, flexible mind, a "big mind" that includes everything. It is the mind that always looks straight ahead, that is not distracted by desire on the left or discomfort on the right. When discomfort does arise, the important point is to refrain from immediately adjusting the posture. Instead, we focus attention on the place of discomfort, acknowledge it, accept it, without trying to push it or force it away. We treat it as if it were a guest. We see if you can sit quietly for another ten seconds without scratching the itch, brushing away the mosquito, or shifting the leg. Then we try another ten seconds. In other words, we don't declare war on the discomfort as if it were an invader. When we do become aware of pain or discomfort, a gracious, noncombative attitude expands our "comfort zone" and helps increase our tolerance for uninvited irritations. Consider how this aware, patient, and accepting attitude toward discomfort might express itself in personal relations, in difficult work situations, and in other areas of life.

—LES KAYE,
Joyously Through the Days

153

Meditation is above all an inner art; it requires a willingness to cultivate a turning inward and resting in that inner arc, that inner focus. At the beginning of your practice when you are building confidence and skills it also requires a willingness to rest in a nondoing state, not trying to fix anything; rather, patiently cultivating a different relationship with yourself and, flowing from that endeavor, with the world you inhabit.

—

Don't spend too much time analyzing your experiences in meditation. I advocate the no-nonsense, don't-complicate-it school of meditation practice. "Do it, don't judge it."

—

Mindfulness is the cultivation of a "choiceless" or "non-choosing" awareness of whatever is happening in the moment. This is awareness without choosing to accept some experiences and reject others, without trying to create any particular state of mind.

—Bob Sharples,
Meditation and Relaxation in Plain English

154

Just as the ocean's salty water
Taken into the clouds turns sweet,
The stable mind works to benefit others;
The poison of objects turns into healing nectar.

—KHENCHEN THRANGU RINPOCHE,
A Song for the King

155

I think the form of intensive retreats is very well suited to our culture because it gives us the chance to slow down, to live in the great beauty of silence, to realistically begin training the mind.

—JOSEPH GOLDSTEIN
IN *The Best of Inquiring Mind*

156

In our pursuit of happiness, it is vital to recognize how few things in the world are subject to our personal control. Other people—family, friends, busy colleagues, and strangers—behave as they wish, in accordance with their own ideas and aims. Likewise, there is little we can do to control the economy, international relations, or the natural environment. So if we base our pursuit of happiness on our ability to influence other people and the world at large, we are almost certainly doomed to failure. What can we control? What freedom do we really have here and now? Our first act of freedom should be to choose our priorities wisely.

—B. ALAN WALLACE,
The Attention Revolution

157

Let us look at spiritual life as many spiritual giants have portrayed it. At the beginning, the work is mostly ours. We must do our part or nothing else will happen. In the middle, increasing purity is both God's and our work together. In the end, God will do it all. Twentieth-century Vedantic mystic Sri Aurobindo added that, in the very, very end, we realize it was God all along.

—MARY JO MEADOW AND KEVIN CULLIGAN,
Christian Insight Meditation

158

The importance of recognizing contemplative *and* psychological practices as "whole body" experiences cannot be overestimated. To fail in this is to be locked into conceptual trajectories, which, although absolutely important, cannot——as every experienced contemplative and psychologist knows all too well—hold the full dimension of human being.

—ANNE CAROLYN KLEIN
IN *Buddhism and Psychotherapy Across Cultures*

159

Bodhisattvas always delight
In teaching the Dharma
In a peaceful,
Comforting way.

—BUDDHA
IN *The Lotus Sutra*

160

To change every moment means to die every moment. On the other hand, it also means to be reborn every moment. Foolish people cling to moments that have already passed by, and in so doing lead futile lives, whereas wise people, understanding that everything changes each instant, apply this principle to their daily lives and live freely.

—DAEHAENG SUNIM,
No River to Cross

161

The Buddha didn't claim the four noble truths were of his own invention. He could spell them out in four reasoned steps, but the source of these steps was a timeless wisdom that predated his or anyone else's discovery of them. He once described the path leading to the cessation of suffering as an "ancient road traveled by the perfectly enlightened ones of the past." When the Buddha gave his first discourse on the four noble truths, he wasn't offering an opinion to the ascetics; he was passing on a law of the universe.

—LIN JENSEN,
Deep Down Things

162

If you get into any difficulty, stop and ask yourself, "Which of the hindrances is this?" Find out what the cause is. Once you know the cause, then you can remember the solution and apply it. If it's sensory desire, just take the attention away from the five senses little by little and apply it to the breath or the mind. If it's ill will, do some loving-kindness. For sloth and torpor, remember "give value to awareness." If it's restlessness and remorse, remember "contentment, contentment, contentment" or practice forgiveness. And if it's doubt, be confident and be inspired by the teachings. Whenever you meditate, apply the solutions methodically. That way, the obstacles you experience won't create long-term barriers. They're things that you can recognize, overcome, and move beyond.

—AJAHN BRAHM,
Mindfulness, Bliss, and Beyond

163

Two strategies for achieving happiness: One is to change the external environment to meet the needs (or wants) of the organism; the other is to change the internal state of the organism to adapt itself to the environment. We can either change the world to satisfy our desires or change our desires by adapting to the world. Both strategies aim at removing the agitation of desires, one by fulfilling them and the other by relinquishing them.

—ANDREW OLENDZKI,
Unlimiting Mind

164

It seems to me that we awaken more profoundly out of hard times than out of the calm times in our life. Crisis and opportunity are indeed one and the same. When we are faced with a setback or difficulty, we always have the opportunity to either label whatever is happening "difficult," "failure," or "crisis"—or not to label it at all and instead see it as "just this." This view of reality, without labels, allows for all kinds of possibilities to arise if we could only trust the moment. Developing such trust is the work of Zen.

—JANET JIRYU ABELS,
Making Zen Your Own

165

The Judge compares all things to each other even though it makes no sense. For example, she might say, "This life is very strange" (as someone once said, "Compared to what?").

Or she might exclaim, "Oh, this kind of snow is much better than that kind of snow." She simply never lets up, which is quite extraordinary when you stop to consider how much work it is.

The Judge doesn't stop there. She then moves on to judge herself as well as the judgments she continually makes. Judging judgments—now there's a good one. It's like a hall of mirrors. Following her whims makes me weary. I wish the Judge would take a little vacation—doesn't she ever get tired of it? Or need a break? I've suggested this to her, but she insists she is passionate about her work.

I've decided now, after listening to her all morning, to just let her do her job. I'll do mine, which is to go straight ahead with the practice and not pay one scrap of attention to her. I'll let her be like the wind blowing by. Let her go ahead and scream; she's just the call of a wild bird to me. Or an airplane flying overhead. Why should I be like a dog that runs after every bone she likes to throw?

➡

She comes out of nowhere and she returns to nowhere, just like everything else.

I bow three times to her.

Now that I think about it, she's actually one of the best teachers I ever had.

Thank you for your teaching, Judge.

—JANE DOBISZ,
One Hundred Days of Solitude

166

To the angry mind there is never any justification for another's actions and always plenty justification for our own.

However, there is another choice here. We can think, "I am acting unskillfully because I am controlled by my anger. Maybe it is the same with the other person. Maybe she is controlled by emotions and is suffering just as much as I am. And further, maybe I have contributed to the situation in some way and I am at least partially responsible. If I really were as perfect as my wounded ego is telling me I am, then there would be no way that person could upset me so much. So maybe I need to look at exactly why I am so upset from the point of view of my own shortcomings rather than hers." A thought process along these lines can help us diffuse the anger in our minds.

—Geshe Tashi Tsering,
Buddhist Psychology

167

No one else can practice the Dharma for us; we have to practice it ourselves. But we do not have to practice it *by* ourselves. We can practice it in the company of other like-minded people who are trying to do the same, and this is the best way—in fact, the only effective way—to practice.

—URGYEN SANGHARAKSHITA,
The Essential Sangharakshita

168

Investigate—find out what the wrong track is, and don't go there again; see it as a snake and avoid it. If you're on the wrong track right now, just be patient and still; you won't stay there for long. Instead of trying to discipline your mind with ill will, fault-finding, guilt, punishment, and fear, use something far more powerful: the beautiful kindness, gentleness, and forgiveness of making peace with life—in short, the *Dhamma* of the Buddha. The longer you live and practice like this, the more pure your heart will become.

———

My own ability in meditation comes from my attitude of saying, "This is good enough," to whatever I'm experiencing. Ability in meditation is all about attitude. When you meditate, be contented and easily satisfied. This is not being lazy.

—AJAHN BRAHM,
The Art of Disappearing

169

Tibetans traditionally talk about three things that need be cultivated in Dharma practice. These might be translated as *play*, *skill*, and *beauty*.

Beauty refers to the rightness of what happens as we exercise the qualities of play and skill in our mind. We can sometimes sense when things are moving in the right way; when we are dealing skillfully and harmoniously with our experience. The beauty aspect is a kind of feedback that confirms this.

Skill includes the idea of power and creativity. It is skill that enables us to catch anger at the moment it arises. And the nearer we get to that point, the greater our skill.

The *play* aspect is the enjoyment involved in our practice. Instead of treating the whole business as a great, heavy, and serious matter, we could treat it more like a game. The way the practice of Dharma works on our minds is something we can enjoy. And we can feel happy about the skill that we gradually acquire.

—RIGDZIN SHIKPO,
Never Turn Away

170

Once you recognize your mind's arguments as thoughts, you can let them dissipate. Be kind to yourself, and give yourself credit even for just remembering to form or return to your intention.

—DEBORAH SCHOEBERLEIN,
Mindful Teaching and Teaching Mindfulness

171

What is called *cessation* must be actualized within our own minds, and we must therefore train in the causes that will lead to its attainment. We must put our understanding into actual practice.

—THE DALAI LAMA,
The Middle Way

172

LIKE A YETI CATCHING MARMOTS.
The Yeti, or Dremo in Tibetan, is a dim-witted mythical
beast said to feed only on marmots. It sees a marmot,
grabs the hapless creature, and then sits on it—saving the
delicious morsel for later. And then the Yeti sees another
marmot and leaps up to snatch it—while the first marmot
makes a quick break for freedom. An image of bumbling,
foolish effort—and the pitfalls of greed.

—PEMA TSEWANG,
Like a Yeti Catching Marmots

173

All day long, remind yourself to be with what is. You can help cultivate this kind of attitude with this gatha: "Breathing in, I let it all go; Breathing out, I let it all be."

—THOMAS BIEN,
Mindful Therapy

174

In every interaction: be careful, be kind.

—

Practice compassion even if no one else does.

—LAMA ZOPA RINPOCHE,
How to Be Happy

175

We do not exist independently from others, so our well-being cannot arise independently of others either. To flourish individually, we must consider the well-being of those around us.

———

We can't help but influence those around us through both our action and our inaction. We are making an impact on the world, whether we want to or not. The last question you may ask yourself is, What would I love to offer to the world, to those around me, and to the environment at large? What kind of a mark would I love to make on the world? Invite this vision into your field of consciousness, embellishing it with as many details as you can think of, and then imagine that this dream is being realized here and now.

—B. ALAN WALLACE,
The Attention Revolution

176

What do you do when you find unpleasant guests are knocking at the door of home? Some thinly disguised versions of greed, hatred, or ignorance. Of course, the guests are usually better presented than this scruffy bunch sounds, because the self does a fair bit of work to make them more presentable to itself.

Practice says a strange thing: So that you can let them go, make mindful room for them. Welcome them in as the brief guests passing through that they really are, not the long-stay tyrants we can easily turn them into. Find out who they are really, so you can know more skillfully how to let them go. The Way is not about drowning in bliss but establishing freedom in every mood, condition, emotion, and belief. And so it has to be about knowing, moment by moment, our actual condition upside-down and inside-out, with an alert, curious, willing attentiveness. Sitting patiently and ungrudgingly with the way things actually are.

—SUSAN MURPHY,
Upside-Down Zen

177

Just understand that birth-and-death is itself nirvana.
There is nothing such as birth and death to be avoided;
there is nothing such as nirvana to be sought.
Only when you realize this are you free from birth
and death.

—DOGEN

IN *The World Is Made of Stories*

178

There are ten corruptions of insight: illumination, knowledge, rapture, calm, bliss, faith, energy, mindfulness, equanimity, and attachment. These corruptions arise in no particular order, and not every meditator will encounter or even notice the presence of each one.

Although there are meditators who can undergo these experiences and not mistakenly believe that they herald the attainment of enlightenment, it is rare for a meditator not to form a subtle attachment to one or all of them. Through the earnest application of mindfulness, or through the interaction with a skilled teacher, it becomes apparent that attachment to these experiences is not the path. When we can look upon these experiences as merely phenomena that rise and fall based upon causes and conditions, when we see that they exhibit the same three characteristics of all experience, we have finally reached the stage of the purification by knowledge and vision of what is the path and what is not the path.

—MATTHEW FLICKSTEIN,
The Meditator's Atlas

179

The repeated reference one finds in Buddhism to resolving "the great matter of birth and death" speaks a language that makes the whole thing sound a little too grand and remote somehow. And while the phrase may very well point to a crucial awakening in a student's pursuit of the Way, I don't think it's a perception that's extraordinary. I think it's more a matter of simplicity than anything else, a freedom from worried spiritual elaboration. Life doesn't require you to make a project out of resolving anything.

—LIN JENSEN,
Together Under One Roof

180

The biggest drawback to spiritual thrill seeking lies not in its potential frustration but in its fulfillment—in actually having some high-voltage spiritual experience.

When thrill seekers have such an experience, they are often convinced that they have had a huge spiritual breakthrough: profound enlightenment, a transformative mystical vision, an encounter with God, an experience of nirvana, a visit to the Pure Land, full-blown *kensho*, etc. This is like thinking someone must be your soulmate because they brought you to a huge orgasm. To spiritual thrill seekers, though, the depth, significance, and authenticity of the experience seem self-evident. How can something so "powerful" be anything but a great spiritual opening? They *must* have achieved something incredible, deeply important, and well beyond "ordinary" spiritual experience.

Spiritual thrill seeking has one other notable quality: it tends to burn itself out.

—Scott Edelstein,
Sex and the Spiritual Teacher

181

It is important to note that mindfulness, in and of itself, is not always an inherent good. The motivation in the mind must be pure for the karma of mindfulness to be wholesome.

—ANYEN RINPOCHE,
Momentary Buddhahood

182

Your pet hindrance is like the most abundant species of snake, one that has caught you many times already. So at the beginning of each sitting remind yourself of that pet hindrance. Alert yourself to its danger. Then you will be on the lookout for it, in the space between the knower and the known, throughout your meditation sitting. Using this method you'll rarely get caught.

—AJAHN BRAHM,
Mindfulness, Bliss, and Beyond

183

Practicing in relationship requires understanding the difference between *detachment* and *nonattachment*. *Detachment* means we cut off our emotional connection to a situation—we turn away or just don't care. *Nonattachment* means that we participate in a situation without a specific demand or expectation for a particular outcome. Detachment may manifest as emotional repression; nonattachment is the fundamental principle of Buddhist practice.

—GRACE SCHIRESON,
Zen Women

184

While all things may be equal from one point of view, one-ness is not the only point of view that counts. In fact, what we call compassion is our assertion that not all things are equal. Kindness is not equal to cruelty; attention is not equal to indifference; a sink full of dirty dishes is not equal to having them washed and put away.

———

It has been said that art is the replacement of indifference with attention. Nuances that we normally overlook, in shape, color, proportion, and so forth, are made the objects of our attention rather than blurring into the background of our perception. Religion could be said to have much the same function, only in religious terms we might say that we replace inattention with reverence.

—BARRY MAGID,
Ending the Pursuit of Happiness

185

The practice of recognizing labels as labels and not self-existent truths is itself also a practice of patience. Through simply being aware of the nature of your own thoughts and actions, you can begin to pacify your problems and obtain peace and happiness. Through doing this, you start to find freedom within your own mind.

—LAMA ZOPA RINPOCHE,
How to Be Happy

186

Certain factions of the mind can be bullies.

And perhaps unlike school bullies, bullying thoughts often come from a misguided attempt to protect you.

But be careful: resistance to the bully does not mean fighting violence with violence, but rather a patient, equanimous challenge to the validity of the bully. By welcoming and owning the bully, you can eliminate the struggle, the hardship, and the self-judgment that can accompany his demands.

The bully is, after all, part of the self.

And now you can enjoy your lunch!

—ARNIE KOZAK,
Wild Chickens and Petty Tyrants

187

There are great feelings of compassion and awe that come from the sense of the immensity of these rounds of rebirths and the vastness of the Buddha's vision. Feeling this and seeing that there is a path out of the suffering brings a strong desire to share that path with others. This feeling is so well expressed by the Zen poet-monk Ryokan:

> O, that my monk's robe were wide enough
> to gather up all the suffering people
> in this floating world.

The practice is never for ourselves alone.

—JOSEPH GOLDSTEIN
IN *The Best of Inquiring Mind*

188

The Zen development theory I offer follows these major stages: (1) idealization, (2) covert clinging to hopes for magical gain, (3) extreme crabbiness at self and other, (4) steadily walking without getting anywhere, (5) experiencing fruition, (6) falling into a well.

And then, of course, the spiral stages repeat.

—DOSHO PORT,
Keep Me in Your Heart a While

189

Meditation, chanting, reading sutras—these are all tools that can be useful under the right circumstances. But I think there's just as much (if not more) Buddhism in giving my wife a hug when she comes home from a long day, in dropping a buck in the homeless woman's cup on the corner, in waiting until everyone gets off the train before trying to push my way inside. And in seeing the Buddha within everyone, and recognizing these relationships, major and minor, as aspects of the dharmakaya, marked by *shunyata* and thus no hindrance, just part of the ebb and flow of emptiness's form.

—JEFF WILSON,
Buddhism of the Heart

190

Recognition and acceptance of what is going on in our mind is not automatic. We are not always aware, in a conscious sense, of how we feel, especially when under pressure to meet a deadline or any of the other demands of our complex lives. Yet a positive response to a disturbing emotion can only begin with an awareness that surfaces through the sea of distractions. The greater our awareness, the more prepared we are to respond creatively to emotions that continually appear.

—LES KAYE,
Joyously Through the Days

191

During meditation, we should not develop a mind that accumulates and holds on to things. Instead we should develop a mind that is willing to let go, to give up all burdens. In our ordinary lives we have to carry the burden of many duties, like so many heavy suitcases, but within the period of meditation such baggage is unnecessary. In meditation, unload as much baggage as you can. Think of duties and achievements as heavy weights pressing upon you. Abandon them freely without looking back.

—

As for the future—the anticipations, fears, plans, and expectations—let that go too. The Buddha once said, "Whatever you think it will be, it will always be something different." This future is known by the wise as uncertain, unknown, and unpredictable. It is often useless to anticipate the future, and in meditation it is always a great waste of time.

—Ajahn Brahm,
Mindfulness, Bliss, and Beyond

192

According to the Buddha, the human world is protected by the "twin guardians," two forces in the mind that watch over and guide moral behavior. The first guardian of the world is *hiri*, a Pali word that connotes conscience, moral intuition, and self-respect. It refers to that within the human psyche which knows the difference between right and wrong, between what is noble and ignoble, between what is worthy of respect and what is not. Each of us has within us an innate moral compass, and it is the view of the Buddhist tradition that religion is not the source of this but rather a form by which it is given expression. The second guardian of the world is *ottappa*, which comprises such notions as social conscience, a cultural or collective sense of morality, and respect for the opinions and the rights of others.

Anything we do that is wholesome will be done with the support and guidance of these two inner guardians. Conversely, everything we do that is unwholesome can only be done when these moral guides are disregarded.

—ANDREW OLENDZKI,
Unlimiting Mind

193

Reverend Dazui, a monk of the Order of Buddhist Contemplatives, encouraged the Buddhist practice of mindfulness as an antidote for a life frittered away by detail. Mindfulness as he taught it was essentially a matter of simplification. He called it "every-minute meditation," and it consisted of five steps, four of which I've repeated here:

1. Do one thing at a time.
2. Pay attention to what you are doing.
3. When your mind wanders to something else bring it back.
4. Repeat step number three a few hundred thousand times.

—LIN JENSEN,
Deep Down Things

194

It's no use hating yourself because you are not the way you would like to be, or beating your head against the wall every time you make a mistake. Doing this only adds more problems to those you already have and does not help you to improve. But having a kind heart toward yourself lightens the pain of failures and faults, provides the space in which you can grow, and lays a good basis for loving relationships with others.

—KATHLEEN MCDONALD,
Awakening the Kind Heart

195

The cultivation of equanimity serves as an antidote to two of the primary afflictions of the mind: attachment and aversion. Attachment includes clinging to serenity—and aversion can arise by regarding all distractions to your practice, including other people, as disagreeable obstacles to your well-being. The essence of equanimity is impartiality. It is equanimity that allows loving-kindness, compassion, and empathetic joy to expand boundlessly. Normally, these qualities are mixed with attachment, but we grow beyond the mental affliction of attachment as we realize that every sentient being is equally worthy of finding happiness and freedom from suffering.

—B. ALAN WALLACE,
The Attention Revolution

196

When there is the first state of resting,
thoughts arise uninterruptedly,
like water rushing down a cliff.
So you think, "Am I not able to meditate?"

The experience of this amount of thoughts arising
is the result of the mind being able to rest a little.
Before you rested in this way,
thoughts arose as they wished,
and you were not aware of the procession of thoughts.

—LAMA SHANG

IN *Mahamudra and Related Instructions*

197

Don't try to figure out what other people want to hear from you; figure out what you have to say. It's the one and only thing you have to offer.

—**Barbara Kingsolver**
in *The Mindful Writer*

198

Reality never happens according to our expectations. Reality is not our little meager idea. And yet we can take responsibility for our efforts. When we show up and befriend ourselves, we start to see more subtly the ways we try to grab on to or get rid of things. But we have to forgive ourselves for being human beings. Zazen is a practice for human beings, not for some super-beings.

—**Taigen Dan Leighton,**
Zen Questions

199

To clarify the mind, doing no harm while giving life to all that is good—there is nothing more essential than this in the teachings of the Buddha.

—

Turning your back on the pain and suffering in the world, or placing yourself as the center of the world and paying no attention to anything else, is not the Buddhadharma. The Buddhadharma does not sell as cheaply as that! The Buddhadharma is the activity of liberating all sentient beings in the whole world—if it's not this, it's not the Buddhadharma.

—SHODO HARADA,
Moon by the Window

200

Stretch a little beyond what seems comfortable.

Sit at least a little most every day.

And plod on.

Forgive yourself your failures, but resume. Fall down, pick yourself up, dust yourself off, and start over again. One teacher liked to say, "Fall down nine times, get up ten." Start over.

That's the practice.

—JAMES ISHMAEL FORD,
If You're Lucky, Your Heart Will Break

201

The many beings are numberless. I vow to save them.
Greed, hatred, and ignorance rise endlessly; I vow to
abandon them.
Dharma gates are countless; I vow to enter them.
The Buddha's way is unsurpassed; I vow to embody it
fully.

Each of these great vows, in fact, is a wonderfully large and impossible proposition when set against our limited human means. Each feels like peering into a vast crater while still trembling behind the safety wire of the reasoning self, who cries, "But, but!" Saving all beings from the heavy sleep of our mind—is that even faintly possible? Finding the creative relationship with our negative states of mind; entering every opportunity to see clearly that opens in front of us; being completely who we are in this life! The safety fence of "reasonable" is necessarily missing at every point in these great vows.

→

Each one is a kind of field of energy, and the crater in reason opened up by each vow is exactly what calls up that energy—it transmutes "unreasonable" into a passionate urge to realize the heart-mind, to encompass all that is. Each vow, like the universe itself, is inexhaustible.

Don't worry—you'll never come to the end of any vow or ever run short of fuel for the fire. Just to contemplate each one is to begin to appreciate at the same moment both the puniness of ordinary human means and that transcendence is a matter that somehow requires this fragile set of bones. How we are is exactly what it takes.

—SUSAN MURPHY,
Upside-Down Zen

202

Focusing on the person who is making you angry is a wonderful meditation. Imagine all the good qualities that that person has in potential, and imagine as you fill him or her with white light that those qualities are actualized. Sometimes it may be emotionally painful to do this with an enemy, but it is painful in a positive way.

—GESHE TASHI TSERING,
Buddhist Psychology

203

Buddhist teacher Shinzen Young clarifies the relationship between pain and suffering with the following equation:

SUFFERING = PAIN x RESISTANCE

Pain comes and goes in life. But that is not yet suffering. Suffering is the product of the pain and our resistance to it. If RESISTANCE equals zero then SUFFERING also equals zero. The more we tighten up against pain, the more we suffer. The more we ease up and open out to the pain, softening to it, allowing and experiencing it, the less we suffer.

—THOMAS BIEN,
Mindful Therapy

204

Sincere love means love without any expectation that the other person will want you, or be nice to you, or do anything at all for you in return. Sincere love means helping someone out of loving-kindness and compassion, simply because that person is suffering and you wish him or her to be free from suffering and to be happy. Whether people thank you or not, you help them because they have a problem and need help. That is the essence of sincere love.

—LAMA ZOPA RINPOCHE,
How to Be Happy

205

As we push through any koan—experiencing great doubt, great faith, and great determination—we find the exact identity between our ordinary consciousness and fundamental openness. Nondual reality includes subject and object, each itself and freely transposing with the other; first this, now that, sometimes one drops away, sometimes the other, sometimes both drop away, sometimes one emerges from the other, sometimes both emerge together—but we *rest* nowhere. Resting nowhere and moving fluidly among these perspectives is the true practice of koan introspection.

—

Doubt and faith travel together. It is our relentless presence to doubt and faith that takes us to the gate of nondual insight. Indeed both the path to the gate and the gate itself are discovered within that relentlessness.

—JAMES ISHMAEL FORD,
Zen Master WHO?

206

Everything is real and not real,
both real and not real,
neither real nor not real—
this is the Buddha's teaching.

—NAGARJUNA
IN *The Middle Way*

207

First a new metaphor: A koan is a kind of technology, a hack for the mind. It strips our opinions and views away. Unlike some other technologies, koans don't work in a linear fashion. They surprise you by transcending the terms on which you took them up. They draw you into a different way of seeing and experiencing your world.

—JOHN TARRANT
IN *The Book of Mu*

208

We don't have to imagine ourselves performing infinite good deeds, establishing Buddhafields, liberating infinite numbers of beings.... It is more practical to take the Bodhisattva as representing a universal, even omnipresent spiritual energy at work in the universe—an energy we get a sense of every now and then. We can't literally think of being a Bodhisattva, but we can be open to the ideal, aspiring to be a channel for that energy within our own particular sphere. That is the most realistic, even the most honest way to see it. We have to stick very close to our actual situation; otherwise we can get lost in unrealistic aspirations.

—

There is so much that can be done if we have the will and the heart to do it.

—URGYEN SANGHARAKSHITA,
The Essential Sangharakshita

209

By sitting in the stillness of zazen, we are focusing our whole being in the here and now. Rather than shutting ourselves off from the rest of the world, we are plunging into the heart of the world. With every breath, we are tuning in to the vital core, tuning in our "receiver," so to speak, to our connectedness with the living universe. Our focus on breathing in and out literally connects us with our own living core and with all living beings—all the human, animal, and plant domains—with whom we share this breath.

—RUBEN L. F. HABITO,
Healing Breath

210

It's important to be skeptical of anything you regard as "yours." Everything from real estate to the living-room sofa to your toothbrush, right down to your very eyeballs and the air you breathe, is borrowed. Anything borrowed must be returned, and it is this attitude of return that informs the modesty and generosity of the Buddha Way.

I hold my entire life on loan in common with everyone else. If I can dispel from mind the vanity of possession and relax my grip on things, passing on whatever comes to hand, I will come in time to know things for themselves and not as belongings of any sort. Ownership is anathema to Zen not because ownership is evil as such, but because ownership is an intrinsically divisive delusion that inevitably leads to grasping and coveting.

To own something is to be owned by it. To free myself, I must let go.

—LIN JENSEN,
Together Under One Roof

211

Guarding is becoming sensitive to conditions that evoke unskillful energies. Many situations in our everyday lives can give rise to these mind states: rushing to get somewhere on time, commuting in heavy traffic, going to bed late and becoming overtired, skipping meals because we are too busy to eat, drinking too much alcohol, not taking enough time to rest, repressing feelings. Guarding our minds is making an effort to avoid these conditions and, when we cannot, paying close attention so that these unskillful qualities do not arise.

—ARINNA WEISMAN AND JEAN SMITH,
The Beginner's Guide to Insight Meditation

212

My next step was to *look at* the people who asked me for money, to make eye contact except when the person was clearly mentally ill and might respond to eye contact with hostility. When I could look panhandlers in the eye, they became human beings, just like me, and I could experience that quivering of the heart that is truly compassion. Sometimes I gave more than a quarter. Once I took a woman with an infant into a market to buy diapers and formula. Sometimes I got "took," but I didn't mind, because having a more open heart was worth so much more to me than money.

—LAURA S.,
12 Steps on the Buddha's Path

213

Zen is not a quest for perfection, nor does it renounce any part of what is. It refuses no part of the world as unholy. Buddha nature pervades the whole universe, indiscriminately. Zen doesn't hold the world at bay but says come home right where you are, just as you are. There is no end to this adventure of arriving.

—SUSAN MURPHY,
Upside-Down Zen

214

Like the proverbial fish that cannot see the water they swim in, we do not notice the medium we dwell within. Unaware that our stories are stories, we experience them as the world.

But we can change the water. When our accounts of the world become different, the world becomes different.

—DAVID R. LOY,
The World Is Made of Stories

215

The Great Perfection takes no sides.

If it takes sides, it is not the Great Perfection.

The Great Seal doesn't negate or affirm.

If there is negation or affirmation, it is not the Great Seal....

In the Great Middle Way, there is no identity at which
to grasp.

If identity is grasped at, then it is not the Great Middle Way.

—MILAREPA

IN *Meditation on the Nature of Mind*

216

I'm not sure that I can claim that all my years of involvement with Buddhism have made me a better person. What I'm most aware of, in fact, is just how less than perfect I am. It is Buddhism that has woken me up to my imperfections and given me the ability to chuckle at my needy little ego's constant attempts to find security and self-aggrandizement in an ever-shifting, largely indifferent world. I can't really hope to keep the precepts, as much as I sincerely wish to do so. I can't even manage to perform my service before the home altar regularly.

I guess there is one advantage to realizing that you're never going to get it right: you do begin to stop expecting everyone else to get it right too, which makes for less frustration when other people turn out to be just as human as you are.

—JEFF WILSON,
Buddhism of the Heart

217

To flourish as a human being is something deeper than having everything go our way in life. Flourishing in this true sense is a process that can continue, through good times and bad, even through the most painful realities of life.

Engendering this flourishing is the primary goal of the Buddhist Sangha.

—RISHI SATIVIHARI,
Unlearning the Basics

218

Do not call it realization or enlightenment; such names will spoil your fun. You are a child of a barbarian. You ought to be satisfied with the name.

—NYOGEN SENZAKI,
Eloquent Silence

219

It is natural and inevitable that we are always working with an imperfect model of reality. It makes a difference, however, to understand the limitations of our constructed system, to see more clearly the consequences of it being both unskillfully and skillfully employed, and to use this knowledge to maximize the well-being available for ourselves and all those around us.

And the Buddhist word for this is *wisdom*.

—ANDREW OLENDZKI,
Unlimiting Mind

220

During my mother's visit, she and I got stuck one time in a daughter-mother knot. It was one of those difficult moments that daughters and mothers have. I stalked down to the laundry room, grabbed the wadded mess of wet clothes from the washer, shook out shirts, pants, and dresses, and with ferocity pinned them to the line. As each piece unfurled, unaccountably, hidden feelings and memories unfolded too—old hurts, bitterness, guilt. All were newly felt—then released into the wind. A sadness opened up, so raw, so clean, and it too was felt, wept through, released, until I started to laugh, and all that was left was love for my mother, growing old and soon to be flying away from me across the continent.

I just can't take my "self" too seriously with all those blouses and pants flapping in the wind. As the breeze picks up, there it is, a loose-limbed dance, not exactly a dance of skeletons, but of bodiless clothes, a chorus line of jeans kicking up a no-self cancan.

—BARBARA GATES
IN *The Best of Inquiring Mind*

221

The universe is dynamic in all dimensions and scales of activity, with every action affecting and generating others in turn.

A Chinese Buddhist metaphor for this view is the Jewel Net of Indra. Imagine a net extending infinitely across horizontal and vertical dimensions of space. Then add more nets crisscrossing on the diagonals. And then imagine an infinite number of these nets crisscrossing every plane of space. At each node in every net, there is a multifaceted jewel which reflects every other jewel in the net. There is nothing outside the Net and nothing which does not reverberate its presence throughout this Net of infinite capacity. The jewels and the infinite links across space are all changing constantly, and always reflecting each other in that process.

—STEPHANIE KAZA
IN *Mindful Politics*

222

I love that *tonglen* is a two-for-one compassion practice. The formal instruction is to breathe in the suffering of others and breathe out kindness, serenity, and compassion. But the effect of repeated practice is that we connect with our own suffering, anguish, stress, discomfort. So as we breathe in the suffering of others concerning a struggle we share with them, we are breathing in our own suffering over that struggle as well. As we breathe out whatever measure of kindness, serenity, and compassion we have to give, we are offering those sublime states to ourselves too. All beings are included.

—TONI BERNHARD,
How to Be Sick

223

Joy comes from appreciation. Appreciation comes from paying attention. Paying attention is the practice of Zen. It's so simple, yet look how I have had to strip away everything, come out here to a cabin in the middle of nowhere, adhere to an unforgiving schedule, and stick it out through all the ups and downs in order to discover it.

It's very humbling.

—JANE DOBISZ,
One Hundred Days of Solitude

224

Each of us is completely responsible for the happiness of every other being. Each of us has this universal responsibility. It's completely up to us. When you work with your mind, what you are doing is the real, ultimate solution for world peace—and not only peace on earth, but for all the beings in all the numberless universes.

—LAMA ZOPA RINPOCHE,
How to Be Happy

225

We all have the capacity to offer the best of ourselves. Sometimes it is not easy, but it is always worth it. No matter the outcome, anyone can change someone's life or help in some small way. What a wonderful practice!

—

The kindness we extend to others ripples out into the universe endlessly.

—CALVIN MALONE,
Razor-Wire Dharma

226

The heart of insight practice is investigating and ultimately eradicating the deeply held belief that there is a permanent and substantial core at the root of our personality around which the attributes of our body and mind cluster.

—MATTHEW FLICKSTEIN,
The Meditator's Atlas

227

Economics that hurt the moral well-being of an individual or a nation are immoral.

—MAHATMA GANDHI
IN *Business and the Buddha*

228

The bodhisattvas all raised their voices together and spoke in verse:

Please do not worry.
After the Buddha's extinction,
In a frightful and evil age
We will teach everywhere.

—FROM *The Lotus Sutra*

—

You are never alone: everywhere, all the time there are numberless buddhas and bodhisattvas surrounding you, loving you, guiding you—after all, that is what they do.

—LAMA ZOPA RINPOCHE,
How to Be Happy

229

Every single action, word, or thought that is motivated by the aspiration to be more kind, to cause less harm, and to create less suffering sets ripples of goodness in motion that can transform your mind into a sea of tranquility and happiness. What's more, this energy, if reinforced and built upon, can lead to untold positive effects for countless others near and far in both time and place. How wonderful!

—TANA PESSO,
First Invite Love In

230

When others out of jealousy
treat me wrongly with abuse and slander,
I will train to take upon myself the defeat
and offer to others the victory.

Whether or not we are at fault, if others slander us or malign us out of jealousy or other motives, instead of harboring resentment, we should respond with a gentle mind. Free of resentment, we should refrain from claiming, for instance, "I am innocent. Others are to blame." Like Langri Thangpa, we should take the defeat upon ourselves. It is said that whenever misfortunes befell another, he would say, "I too am in him."

—CHEKAWA YESHE DORJE
IN *Essential Mind Training*

231

Applying mindfulness gets easier over time. At first, just focus on increasing your attention during one or two specific activities while moving through the others normally. Also, remember that mindfulness is not a function of speed, and "mindful" does not itself mean "slow." As much as possible, maintain a sense of humor and perspective in the process—whatever happens.

—DEBORAH SCHOEBERLEIN,
Mindful Teaching and Teaching Mindfulness

232

Healing insight into the cause of our suffering is not just a cognitive matter. Intellectual insight is not enough. Liberating insight into the cause of suffering involves our whole being—intellect and emotions, heart and mind—everything. In the language of psychotherapy, it is the process of "working through," of continuing to bring accepting awareness to problems as they recycle through a series of clinical sessions.

The process of working through may be compared to untying a knot. To be effective in untying a knot, it helps to have an attitude of calm and patience. One must not be in a hurry. Some knots are small and simple. A pull here, a tug there, and *voilà*, the knot is untied. A larger knot will require much more time and patience. It may well not be untied in one sitting but will call for a patient process of returning to it again and again, tugging a little bit here, pulling a little bit there. Eventually it will yield. Eventually, everything yields to the gentle power of mindfulness.

—Thomas Bien,
Mindful Therapy

233

Shikantaza means "nothing but sitting." Just sitting is a matter of sinking into one's bones and sinews and facing the bare ground of mind. Each thing that arises is allowed to come and go, within the one who sits. What comes and goes there—that too is gradually more empty and clear, like the one who sits. Who is it? Nothing sticks to that one. And nothing is clung to. Is it you? It seems to have no name, and to be far wider than the one called by your name. Attending to the breath is the way in, then that too falls away from prominence in the state of brightly alert attention that opens, directed to no object, attached to no content.

—SUSAN MURPHY,
Upside-Down Zen

234

All appearances to the contrary, we humans are host to an inherent sense of fairness that when neglected or denied reasserts itself of its own accord. If you or I cheat or finagle others out of things that are rightfully theirs, we subject ourselves to a regret that regardless of the degree of our denial works its way into our hearts. Regret is an ethical corrective, an agent of what Buddhists call *karma*. Regret is a medicine offered a sick heart as a means of healing itself. It can be a bitter remedy, but I'm grateful for the healing it brings, however painful that may at times be.

—LIN JENSEN,
Deep Down Things

235

Let compassion guide me,
humility hold me,
and courage temper my wild mind.

—KATHLEEN WILLIS MORTON,
The Blue Poppy and the Mustard Seed

236

As the saying goes, the only way beyond is through. The way to overcome something is not to avoid it but to move into it.

—

Mindfulness can help you to appreciate the richness and variation that is present in the sameness of things.

—ARNIE KOZAK,
Wild Chickens and Petty Tyrants

237

Meditation practice helps break uncreative habit patterns in two ways. By increasing awareness, it helps the mind bring habits into consciousness. By recognizing the habitual reaction as it starts to arise, we have the opportunity to break the short circuit by choosing to bring our attention to the situation and to create an appropriate response, rather than falling back on words or action that might have worked in the past. In addition, because meditation is the practice of "letting go" as well as the practice of awareness, habit patterns may simply fade from the mind without our conscious recognition. Intrinsic in the fading, stubbornness is diminished, replaced by a feeling of mental flexibility and freedom.

—LES KAYE,
Joyously Through the Days

238

Realization is not something we can will, it is something that happens to us. It's no good to try and pretend that we can simply suspend our judgments and be less critical or angry than we actually are. That's a big danger in spiritual practice. We think we're supposed to be compassionate and non-judgmental, so we put on a facade and try to act that way. We indeed can and should control our behavior, but we can't control our feelings, still less our unconscious beliefs. Control may be useful up to a point—it's good to know that we can control our actions and behave well regardless of how we feel inside—but unless we're completely honest about how angry and judgmental we really are, and are willing to sit with those thoughts and feelings and label them carefully over and over, we are never going to engage them in a meaningful way. We can't will the change, we can only be honest, pay attention, and let any change happen as it happens in its own time.

—BARRY MAGID,
Ending the Pursuit of Happiness

239

At one point in my daughter's stormy adolescence, she refused to speak to me for six months. She did not respond with even a word to any overtures I made.

I felt frustrated and upset; as a psychologist, I had an investment in the value of talking as a means to work things out and pride in my ability to empathize and communicate. I tried everything I could think of to break the impasse, but without success. Finally I lost my patience and, utterly helpless, I cried out to her:

"I don't know what to do! I've tried writing letters, and that didn't work. I've tried active listening, and that didn't work. I've tried being silent, I've tried making contracts and agreements, and none of them worked. I've tried everything I can think of and I'm completely out of ideas! I'm stumped! I HAVE NO IDEA HOW TO COMMUNICATE WITH YOU!"

At that, my daughter turned to face me and looked me straight in the eye.

"Good!" she said. "NOW we can make a start!"

So we did.

—Robert Meikyo Rosenbaum, *Walking the Way*

240

The Story of the Little Salt Doll

Once upon a time, there was a little doll made of salt who had made a long pilgrimage on dry land. One day she came to the sea, which was something she had never seen before. Here she found herself confronting a phenomenon she felt she could not possibly know or understand. There she was, a little solid doll of salt, standing on firm ground, watching another sort of ground that was not firm at all, but was moving and insecure and noisy and strange and unknown. She felt she could never get to know or understand it.

Nevertheless, the little doll walked right up to the edge of the sea and asked, "What are you?"

The sea replied, "I am me."

The doll said, "I've never seen anything like you before. I don't know you at all. I'd like to, though. Please help me and tell me how I can come to know you."

The sea answered, "Touch me."

The little doll shyly put forth her foot and touched the water. Oh, how different! She felt a unique thing happening, and knew she was somewhat lighter, something she had never experienced before. But it did give her the feeling that the sea could be knowable. She withdrew her leg, and as

➥

it came out of the water, she could see that her toes had disappeared.

"What have you done to me?" she cried.

The sea replied kindly, "You have given something in order to understand."

At first the doll was disconcerted and wasn't sure just how profitable this exchange really was. But she *did* feel better, and went into the sea again, a little further, so that she would understand more deeply. Once again the sea took away more of her salt. Strangely enough, this gave her a liberated feeling, so she went farther and farther into the sea. At each succeeding moment she seemed to understand more deeply, although all the while she was losing more of her salt. Her determination kept her going, and so did that ultimate question, "But what *is* the sea?"

Finally, a big wave engulfed her, and as it dissolved the rest of her salt, the little doll cried out in great happiness, "Now I know what the sea is... *It is I!*"

—ELAINE MACINNES,
The Flowing Bridge

241

Letting go is itself faith. Without faith, you can't let go.

—DAEHAENG SUNIM,
No River to Cross

242

Remember that even when you are interrupted during your meditation, you still have a choice: you can get angry and frustrated or, more beneficially, you can deal with the interruption, settle yourself, and go back to the practice.

—BOB SHARPLES,
Meditation and Relaxation in Plain English

243

Insight is vital to experience the complete annihilation of aversion, attachment, and ignorance. Concentration will temporarily suppress the deluded minds—while we are concentrated—but it will not destroy the root of the three poisons.

—GESHE TASHI TSERING,
Emptiness

244

The heart must break completely open so that everything may be here, fully itself, at last. It's said that until you've wept deeply, you haven't meditated. Tears can be the first sign of grace.

—

Somehow, profound limitation is a doorway to boundless freedom.

—Susan Murphy,
Upside-Down Zen

245

We can say thank you to the shadows that make us appreciate the light that much more, and learn to use all our gifts appropriately and in the spirit of gratitude.

—

Our own efforts toward deeper insight and understanding can only take place within an infinite matrix of supportive actions by others.

How lucky we are to live in such an open-ended universe, where we can receive what we need from others and contribute toward the happiness and awakening of one another.

—JEFF WILSON,
Buddhism of the Heart

246

A student of Zen is perfectly happy to take a nap but doesn't perceive ease as inherently preferable to effort.

——

I find myself clinging to beliefs when I don't trust myself to do otherwise.

——

Every moment calls one into being anew.

—LIN JENSEN,
Together Under One Roof

247

The absolute is not light, as we might think, but darkness, for it is unknowable and opaque. It is this unknowable darkness that is light. The relative, or worldly, is not darkness, as we might think, but light, for it is seen and knowable. This knowable light is darkness. Light and darkness are not separate but in harmony.

—JANET JIRYU ABELS,
Making Zen Your Own

248

Going through difficult, unwanted experiences does not have to be terrible or unbearable. Problems can be opportunities for learning and growth; they can even be beautiful and inspiring. A friend who had cancer when he was just in his twenties said it was the best thing that ever happened to him. Through that experience, he resolved old problems with his family and developed closer ties with them. He also became interested in the spiritual path, learned meditation, and even decided to become a monk so he could devote himself fulltime to spiritual study and practice. There are many cases of people who have made constructive changes in their lives after going through a difficult time.

—KATHLEEN McDONALD,
Awakening the Kind Heart

249

Nondual reality includes subject and object, each itself and freely transposing with the other; first this, now that—sometimes one drops away, sometimes the other, sometimes both drop away, sometimes one emerges from the other, sometimes both emerge together—but we rest nowhere. Resting nowhere and moving fluidly among these perspectives is the true practice of koan introspection—helping us on our way.

—JAMES ISHMAEL FORD,
If You're Lucky, Your Heart Will Break

250

It is indeed a fault for one
Who returns anger for anger;
Not giving anger for anger,
One wins a double victory.
He behaves for the good of both:
Himself and the other person.
Knowing well the other's anger,
He is mindful and remains calm.
In this way he is healing both:
Himself and the other person.
The people who think "He's a fool"
Just don't understand the Dharma.

—BUDDHA

IN *Unlimiting Mind*

251

Buddhist practice reveals that compassion is the only rational response to the confusion and affliction that infuse the human realm.

—NOAH LEVINE
IN *Mindful Politics*

252

We're so interconnected that someone who, let's say, is on retreat or working alone to restore a tract of wilderness is actually affecting us all, not just because it's arithmetically true that one-billionth of the world is getting cleaner but because there's a coarising dynamic there. The whole is intrinsically altered, and each of us with it.

—JOANNA MACY
IN *The Best of Inquiring Mind*

253

When you understand that the senses have nothing to do with you, you naturally give up your concern for them and allow them to disappear—even the aches and pains. How can you be in great pain and still smile? If the senses have nothing to do with you, neither does the pain. And if the pain has nothing to do with you, it's not important to you, and you can simply let it be. You only pay attention to something if you think it's important.

—

Remember that this is the Buddhist path, a path of investigation. You won't be able to let go by using willpower; only by understanding things and tracing them back to their source can you let them go.

—AJAHN BRAHM,
The Art of Disappearing

254

Through the practice of mindfulness, we develop a state of mental stability and stillness. This is merely a state of tranquility and not the recognition of the mind's true nature. Therefore, we need to go further and practice *nonminding*. This does not mean that we lose the faculty of mindfulness; rather, it means seeing the nature of the mind, seeing the emptiness of even mindfulness itself.

—KHENCHEN THRANGU RINPOCHE,
A Song for the King

255

Accept your mind and its states. If you are being reasonably accepting of your mind states that's probably a good direction. Mind states are, after all, what we have as humans, they are what we have to embrace and forgive and love, as they are.

Trying to achieve a certain state implies reaching for something not present, living in a projected future world. So no need to try. I know that some of the old teachers said to try hard, but what did they know? You have to truly appear in your own life. Then there is no question of effort or trying.

—JOHN TARRANT
IN *The Book of Mu*

256

Life is in the laboring.

—HAWAIIAN PROVERB
IN *Saltwater Buddha*

257

In the context of our lay practice, the precepts are not so much vows of conduct or rules of behavior as a way of bearing witness to life as it is. We bear witness to the evils enumerated in the precepts the way we bear witness to the reality of old age and death. Witnessing does not preclude or replace the need to do what we can to ameliorate suffering. We do all we can to heal the sick and ease the pain of dying. But we do not imagine it our task to eliminate the fact of sickness, old age, or death from the world, nor do we condemn life itself for including these elements. We do not hate life for including suffering nor do we bitterly resign ourselves to its reality.

We bear witness to the reality of killing all around us, and acknowledge that our life is inevitably grounded in the killing of other life, plant and animal. We bear witness to the reality of theft and inequality in the world, and acknowledge that what we posses and enjoy and use to make our own life secure is gained at the expense of those less fortunate than ourselves. We bear witness to the reality of sexuality, which, fueled by unconscious fantasy and desire, will always contain transgressive elements that resist domestication and erupt in ways that disrupt our ideals of intimacy and mutuality. We bear witness to how our basic human need for love

➥

divides the world into those who are special to us and those to whom we long to be special. We bear witness to all the ways our own personal history of suffering has led us to distrust one another and to distrust life itself, causing us to separate ourselves and withhold our wholehearted participation in life out of fear of being disappointed and hurt once again. Fundamentally, we bear witness to the reality of our own needs, desires, and vulnerabilities and the reality of our being creatures who exist simultaneously in the realms of separation and embeddedness.

A changing, interconnected world whiplashes us between our experience of ourselves as separate individuals and as participants in a seamless whole. We must come to terms with both sides of our nature. Practice will not lead us into a state of harmony by eliminating some aspect of who we are.

—BARRY MAGID,
Nothing Is Hidden

258

Try not to overvalue yourself and want everybody else also to treat you that way.

—JOHN OF THE CROSS
IN *Christian Insight Meditation*

259

The Middle Way finds its center not on the temporal stage of human history but in the cosmic time of vast emptiness.

—MARK UNNO
IN *Buddhism and Psychotherapy Across Cultures*

260

When we sit with some idea to calm down and cool out, or to get some new perspective on a situation, that might be chasing after self. Or perhaps that is simply just our practice. One teacher, Jingqing, said that he was "almost not confused by self." Something about that is very appealing. Saying "I'm not at all confused by self" might be a little too much. If you say that, some confusion appears. We may easily get seduced by the grand idea of perfection, of not ever being confused at all. Such perfection is a misleading, inhuman ideal. I instead aspire simply to "I'm almost not confused by self."

As a great American yogi (Yogi Berra) said, with one of my favorite Dharma utterances, "If the world were perfect, it wouldn't be."

—Taigen Dan Leighton,
Zen Questions

261

This wisdom through realization
does not come from anywhere,
does not go anywhere,
and does not reside anywhere.

The wisdom of realization and what it realizes,
both dissolve into the nonconceptual essence of
    phenomena
without the arrogance of identifying it as the essence.

—LAMA SHANG
IN *Mahamudra and Related Instructions*

262

The spiritual path is a subtle one, and a good guide is important.

—

My own teacher once told me that awakening is always an accident; and I tell my own students this today. There is no obvious causal relationship between nondual insight and anything we might do or not do. But if awakening is an accident, certain practices can help us become accident-prone.

—JAMES ISHMAEL FORD,
Zen Master WHO?

263

When a difficult situation arises, you acknowledge the difficulty but you do not personalize it. You do not add in to the mix a feeling of "Why is it always me?" You don't take a hurricane personally as though the storm sought you out. Similarly, you can come to view the acts of others in a less personal way. You know that the actions of others are also the results of impersonal forces, just like a hurricane. You see in each harmful act the suffering of the person who does it, including the suffering of parents and others who have contributed to the suffering in that person. What is more, you adopt the same attitude toward your own actions. When you look back on your life and see some of your actions and choices as mistakes, you know that you were doing the best you could with the limited understanding you had at that time, and with all the suffering that was within you. To get angry at yourself or at someone else only prolongs and exacerbates this situation.

—THOMAS BIEN,
Mindful Therapy

264

As our practice deepens and we become more transparent to ourselves, we deepen our awareness of our many unhealed wounds—wounds of unsettled issues, of broken relationships—as well as the wounds of others and of Earth. And the balm that can heal all of these wounds, here and now, lies in each breath we breathe.

Picture a mother gently blowing her warm breath on a child's wounded knee and, in some mysterious but discernible way, healing the child in the process. In the same way, when we entrust our lives to the breath in zazen, we can actually sense that mother's breath on the wounds of our being—and on the wounds of Earth itself. The eyes of the heart open, and the powerful compassion working within and through us pours out toward all sentient beings with whom we share that breath.

—RUBEN L. F. HABITO,
Healing Breath

265

There are five basic precepts, or principles of living, that the Buddha prescribed for everyone. These precepts are a guide to behaviors that are either to be avoided, because they lead to unfortunate consequences, or to be cultivated, because they support spiritual development. By following these precepts, our actions and speech are aligned with those of enlightened beings. This alignment helps to foster states of mind that lead to the realization of ultimate truth. As you will discover, the precepts reflect a depth of spiritual practice that may not be initially apparent.

The first precept:
Avoid killing and act with reverence toward all forms
of life.

The second precept:
Avoid stealing and cultivate generosity.

➥

The third precept:
Avoid sexual misconduct and be considerate
in intimate relationships.

The fourth precept:
Avoid lying and relate what is true while remaining
sensitive to the potential impact of all communication.

The fifth precept:
Avoid intoxicants, which confuse the mind and cause
heedless behavior, and ingest only those substances
that are nourishing and supportive of peaceful abiding.

—MATTHEW FLICKSTEIN,
The Meditator's Atlas

266

For whom emptiness is tenable
for him everything becomes tenable;
for whom emptiness is untenable
for him everything becomes untenable.

—NAGARJUNA
IN *The Middle Way*

267

All true human beings are unknown, but some human beings' stories are more untold than others. That "unknown" is historic, karmically regrettable, and must be mourned. The Buddhist bodhisattva of compassion, Kuan Yin, listens also to all the untold stories and hears all the cries of all the silenced women, and everyone else besides. This returns us to the deeper "unknown," that vast reverberant fertile ground that fills us all, trees and clouds and we ourselves, and can be filled by all of us. It leaves nothing out.

—SUSAN MURPHY,
Upside-Down Zen

268

The wonder I feel at there being *something* rather than nothing is so large it goes beyond my calculation, beyond the possibility of my making an explanation, far beyond my understanding. That a parcel of vain strivings should appear in this world and be able to experience love, life, loss, beauty, growth—it is beyond my ability to ever fully comprehend. And that it should be embraced by infinite wisdom and compassion beyond the self and delivered to awakening and bliss—it is truly wondrous.

My only hope of expressing these feelings is through the *nembutsu*, the voice of buddha-nature itself.

—JEFF WILSON,
Buddhism of the Heart

269

Cultivate the determination to use your Dharma practice when the mind is agitated. Each time you realize that you have missed an opportunity to practice because you have failed to recognize a disturbance in the mind, regret it and renew your aspiration and determination to recognize all future mental afflictions and conceptual thoughts.

—ANYEN RINPOCHE,
Momentary Buddhahood

270

"How can 'I' go beyond self-consciousness?"

Katagiri Roshi said, "Already you are stuck."

———

A student said, "Sometimes when I'm angry, I'll go and sit zazen. It helps me calm down and process what I'm angry about."

Katagiri Roshi looked down at the floor and grumbled, "Don't use zazen in that way."

———

"Fighting with me is like fighting with tofu."

—DAININ KATAGIRI
IN *Keep Me in Your Heart a While*

271

We have to experience *in the body* how our unwillingness to forgive feels. Staying with the experience in the body is not that easy, because often the sensations that we feel are not particularly pleasant. However, the trick is to bring the mindset of curiosity—just wanting to know what resistance actually feels like. One way to do this is to ask the koan question, *"What is this?"* This is not asking what the resistance is *about*; it's asking what it is. And the only real answer to this question is the actual experience of the present moment itself. The only real answer is *just this*.

—Ezra Bayda
in *Mindful Politics*

272

To liberate ourselves from every speck of fear, we have to know that abundant, huge, wide-open mind. Then we can see the world. We will encounter sickness, calamity, and death. Those are the real things of life. But when we receive it all naturally, our fear is resolved.

—SHODO HARADA,
Moon by the Window

273

In realization one enters into the source, the mind essence. In understanding, one comes out of the oneness, and the mind can work within dualism. Those who have attained realization always know how to return to the source. Therefore, even though their minds can function in dualism, their manner is playful. Sometimes they venture into dualism on purpose, to lead others into the wisdom of the universe.

—NYOGEN SENZAKI,
Eloquent Silence

274

There is a discovery we Western practitioners of Buddhism have come to, somewhat reluctantly, as we have gained more experience in practice, particularly meditation practice. What first drew us, and may continue to draw us, was Buddhism's promise of liberation from suffering, and from the painful sense of incompleteness and limited satisfaction in life. And most of us were not disappointed. We did find a path and a liberation in Buddhadharma that we have not found anywhere else. That is why we continue to practice. But as time has gone on, we have discovered something else about practice: it is not immune from our personal history, our character, our inner conflicts, and our defensive styles.

—

Precisely through the fear and hurt and anger we have contracted around and tried to deny and avoid, we can find freedom, ease, unshakable peace, and a deep, deep joy.

—JACK ENGLER
IN *Buddhism and Psychotherapy Across Cultures*

275

Night rain washes the mountain cliffs,
the dawn greens soaked through.
Sitting, I meditate on emptiness
as fresh breezes fill the temple.
Words are inherently empty and yet
still I am fond of brush and ink.
My mind like ashes after the fire and yet
still I am tied to the world.
Window bamboo—empty mind;
courtyard pine—innate purity.
The trunk of this lofty green tree
neither inherently form nor nonform.
Between bell and fish-drum
I have yet to grasp the essence of Dharma:
Yet I get a whiff of its fragrance
as if I were aboard the Ship of Compassion.

—MIAOHUI
IN *Zen Women*

276

Fairness calls upon us to share the earth equally with its many beings in an attitude of mutual interest wherein no distinction is drawn between self and other. The Buddha identified a source of suffering in the failure to share. Suffering, the Buddha taught, is an inevitable consequence of the human predilection toward chasing after things. When my outlook is shrunk to the scale of personal greed, my place in the world shrinks to the same meager scale. It is then that I call upon the force and intention of the vow I have taken to save the many beings. What I ask of that vow is to pry open the clenched fist of greed and let fall from my grasp whatever I've managed to get hold of.

—LIN JENSEN,
Deep Down Things

277

When there is this, there is that,
When there is not this, there is not that.
From the arising of this, that arises.
From the ceasing of this, that ceases.

———

Looking after oneself, one looks after others.
Looking after others, one looks after oneself.

—BUDDHA
IN *Unlimiting Mind*

278

There it is again: "Not for me."
It's for all beings.
Sinking, sinking, sinking in.
Down into my bones and heart.
I'm not a perfect bodhisattva.
I have a long way to go, but it's all right.
I'm going.

—JANE DOBISZ,
One Hundred Days of Solitude

279

The real world has a potency that the world of idealized images will never touch. In the real world—where interdependence occurs every single moment—we are ourselves. In the real world we are ordinary. And the more ordinary we get, the more extra-ordinary we become.

—ETHAN NICHTERN,
One City

280

We cannot lose by being generous.

—ARINNA WEISMAN AND JEAN SMITH,
The Beginner's Guide to Insight Meditation

281

There are times in some meditators' practice when their mind is as crazy as an intoxicated bull elephant charging around smashing everything. In such situations don't use force to subdue your raging bull elephant of a mind. Instead use loving-kindness/letting go: "Dear crazy mind of mine, the door of my heart is fully open to you no matter what you ever do to me. You may destroy or crush me, but I will give you no ill will. I love you, my mind, no matter what you ever do." Make peace with your crazy mind instead of fighting it. Such is the power of authentic loving-kindness/letting go that in a surprisingly short time, the mind will be released from its rage and stand meekly before you as your soft mindfulness gently strokes it, "There mind, there..."

—AJAHN BRAHM,
Mindfulness, Bliss, and Beyond

282

The writer D. H. Lawrence said somewhere that you can get to heaven in a single leap but you will leave a devil in your place. It is like that. You can experience a sudden realization and begin to open the eye of insight, but if you hoped that might keep you safe from all subsequent human messiness and frailty, you will leave a devil in the very place you vacated for heaven.

That "devil" is the energy of unacknowledged shadow.

The people we love best stand to know far more about the disowned dark or difficult aspects of personality we may leave behind us in our leap to heaven than we ever will—after all, they're the ones left bearing its weight.

As the practice of sitting deepens we generally find ourselves growing much more tender toward other beings. To sit deeply is an act of becoming less defended and strategic, and more vulnerable, embodied, impermanent—more here.

—SUSAN MURPHY,
Upside-Down Zen

283

It's important to recognize that experiencing resistance to spiritual discipline is not a "bad" thing, to be conquered and eliminated. Neither is it something to be ignored. It is an integral, predictable part of the process. When there is strong attachment to a particular story in the mind about who we and others are, there is naturally going to be resistance to the dis-illusionment process. Carefully, respectfully exploring it is itself following the path.

—RISHI SATIVIHARI,
Unlearning the Basics

284

For me, the most effective way of being in the world is to move in the direction of the stream of the Dharma. But one is not automatically "in the stream of the Dharma." That's where practice comes in. Meditation, devotion, Dharma studies, cause-and-effect studies, chopping wood and carrying water, and more meditation yet are the ancient and modern and future paths of entrance into the timeless truths of Buddha, Dharma, Sangha.

—GARY SNYDER
IN *The Best of Inquiring Mind*

285

Compliance masquerades as nonselfcenteredness, sub-mission as devotion, masochism as aspiration. The key to breaking out of this pattern is to acknowledge our own role in creating it.

—

The corollary to an unhealthy *submission* to others is an unhealthy *devotion* to others at the expense of one's own legitimate emotional and physical needs—a parody of com-passion that I have called *vowing to save all beings minus one*. As I have discussed earlier, we may enlist our practice and our attempts at being compassionate in the service of a curative fantasy of eliminating our own neediness and vulnerability. Unable to face need in ourselves, we project it out into the world. We attribute it to all those *others* who are in need of our love, service, and compassion, all the while denying that we ourselves might be in exactly the same condition.

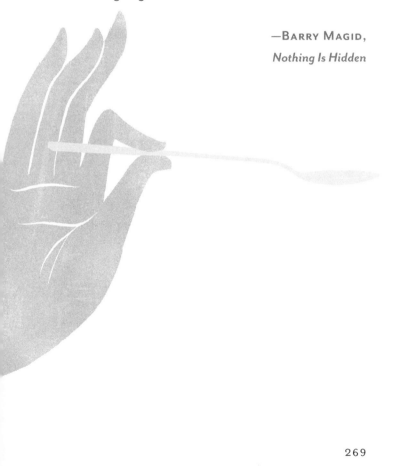

Breaking out of reactive cycles may be a better way of understanding compassion than a picture of endless one-directional giving.

—BARRY MAGID,
Nothing Is Hidden

286

"How do I become a better writer?"

"Just write."

"And then what?"

"Keep writing."

"And then eventually...?"

"You write."

"Until?"

"Until you have written something."

"Then what?"

"You get up out of bed the next morning and write some more."

This is my version of a Zen koan.

—DINTY W. MOORE,
The Mindful Writer

287

Our identities are constructed from what we detest as well as what we love.

—

Our deepest fear is rooted in a compulsion to secure what cannot be secured.

—

Open up and focus on giving to the world rather than taking from it, trusting in it rather than trying to protect yourself from it.

—DAVID R. LOY,
The World Is Made of Stories

288

When a fool pretends to be clever,
he looks all the more foolish.

———

There is no suffering like anger;
there is no penance like patience.

———

You can beat the lake with a stick,
but it won't matter to the fish.

—TIBETAN PROVERBS IN
Like a Yeti Catching Marmots

289

New students sometimes ask me why they need to bother with sitting meditation. They would be much happier meditating as they walk about during the day. Couldn't they just practice in everyday life? How wonderful it would be if we could do that. Unfortunately, it is the most difficult practice of all. It's undoubtedly easier to get our first inspiration and connection through sitting meditation. We can then go on to practice in everyday life. But we would be very foolish to try to replace one with the other.

—RIGDZIN SHIKPO,
Never Turn Away

290

Cultivating kindness can prompt inner compassion as well as the recognition and expression of compassionate acts toward others. This, in turn, helps relieve pain and supports happiness.

—**DEBORAH SCHOEBERLEIN**,
Mindful Teaching and Teaching Mindfulness

291

In our normal ways of living there is a disparity between appearance and reality, and it is this that brings our deep anxiety and fear. Through practice and study, appearance and reality can gradually be brought together, and when they coincide, even for a moment, *that* is the realization of emptiness and joy.

—**JEREMY HAYWARD**,
Warrior-King of Shambhala

292

With no familiar or clearly discernible mind, it's impossible to know who I am, because whoever I thought I was turns out not to be me at all. That moment of self-vacancy, of not knowing who I am, is, for all its fleeting uncertainties, the very threshold of the Buddha Refuge. And the reason this refuge is initially frightening is that it can't be sorted out or understood or identified in any of the mind's familiar ways. Refuge comes without a tag attached. It resists being anything in particular and seems to float among endlessly shifting possibilities. It can't be fixed in place by thought and won't hold still the way an *idea* of myself can be fixed and held still. Refuge is always melting down or burning itself up or dissolving like sugar in water.

—LIN JENSEN,
Together Under One Roof

293

Birth and death are fruitful in the manner in which they undercut the complacency of who we think we are, in the way in which they shake us up and make us question ourselves. If we let them, they can strip away the layers of identity that imprison us, exposing us to the groundlessness that is the bedrock of the Buddha's vision.

—MARK EPSTEIN,
Going on Being

294

Listen to the actions of the Cry Regarder.
How well he responds in every region.
His great vow is as deep as the sea,
Unfathomable even after eons.

—BUDDHA
IN *The Lotus Sutra*

295

One teacher said that the true goal of Zen practice is the perfection of character, the work of becoming who you really are. Don't be misled by the word "perfection." Like housework, perfection is never finished with us. We are all, without exception, its works in progress. This is the work of becoming genuine, a willingness to be more whole in every moment and condition that presents itself.

—SUSAN MURPHY,
Upside-Down Zen

296

Certainly, as I look at myself honestly, relentlessly, in the spirit of not-knowing, frankly I find it impossible to discern any part of me that isn't formed by conditions ranging from my genetic makeup to my ongoing encounters with events and people. I am this because of that. And the "that" that makes "this" changes in a heartbeat—who I am changes, sometimes slightly, sometimes dramatically, with the very next addition of experience.

As I experience it all, it seems we are all part of a great current flowing from some unknown source to some unknown end, like a river on its way to an ocean. All we know with anything even approaching certainty is this moment itself. And we need to notice what we find here.

To work the image a bit, here is the water, of course, rushing on. But there are many other things, as well. Bits of this and that, sticks and pebbles, whatever. Sometimes a bit of brush gets caught toward the edge of the river, and various things collect together in a swirl. This little eddy of stuff is me. Another is you. Just as real as can be. And just as temporary. For me a swirling eddy of Jamesishness. Then somewhere along the line something will happen and the

➡

eddy of stuff that is James will disappear, but the current will continue rushing on, taking new shapes, new forms, each for a moment, before again resuming that great flow from dark to dark.

—JAMES ISHMAEL FORD,
If You're Lucky, Your Heart Will Break

297

Letting everything come and go naturally within the scope of self-recognition; this is the process of auto-purification in empty luminosity.

—KEITH DOWMAN,
Natural Perfection .

298

The poet W. H. Auden has said, "Our claim to own our bodies and our world / is our catastrophe." How can we claim ownership of something that's constantly changing? What does it tell us about the nature of the claim? A deluded mind believes a manifestation to be a thing-in-itself, whereas Buddhist teachings point out that a manifestation is an event. A thing is perceived by the deluded mind to be solid and self-abiding; an event is seen by a mind informed by prajna as a resultant outcome of a certain process. To see oneself truly and authentically, as an *event*—an ever-changing process—rather than a thing-in-itself is the greatest act of re-imaging.

—Mu Soeng,
The Heart of the Universe

299

Consider this passage about an instance when the Buddha was cut by a stone splinter:

> Severe pains assailed him—bodily feelings that were painful, wracking, sharp, piercing, harrowing, disagreeable. But the Buddha endured them, mindful and clearly comprehending, without becoming distressed.

I take this as a reminder that the equanimity and joy we see in the many images of him is within the reach of every one of us.

—TONI BERNHARD,
How to Be Sick

300

The Blessed One uttered these verses:

Many people, frightened with fear,
take refuge in the mountains,
or in forests, or in parks,
or in the shrines of sacred trees.

But this isn't the best refuge;
it isn't the most excellent one.
Recourse to this refuge doesn't
release one from all suffering.

Whoever takes refuge in the Buddha,
in the Dharma, and in the community,
sees, with his wisdom,
the four noble truths—

suffering, the arising of suffering,
its destruction, and how to get beyond it—
and he sees the noble eightfold path,
bestowing safety and leading to nirvana.

➥

This is the best refuge,
this is the most excellent one.
Recourse to this refuge
releases one from all suffering.

—FROM *Divine Stories*

301

There is no magic trick to ridding ourselves of negative emotions. We must confront and overcome them through internal analysis and meditation and with a great deal of patience; it is a slow process. Realizing the destructive nature of the negative emotions, such as anger, and understanding that their causes always lie latent in our minds, we begin the practice of reducing them and lessening their influence in our lives.

—GESHE TASHI TSERING,
Buddhist Psychology

302

People sometimes misunderstand renunciation as being fed up with life. When they struggle for success in the world and fail, running into all sorts of problems, they become discouraged and, out of desperation, say they are renouncing everything. That's not the kind of renunciation we are talking about. That is defeatism. True renunciation is grounded in a deep understanding of the nature of suffering and cyclic existence.

—THE DALAI LAMA,
The Middle Way

303

When consciousness is stripped down there is a velvety, vibrant quality to it—everything is alive and sparkling and also I am you. It's unlikely that you can get to this by a harsh method. As far as we can say that a dream has a basic nature, the basic nature of consciousness is something like empathy and a boundary-less love.

—JOHN TARRANT
IN *The Book of Mu*

304

There is an old story originating with Shantideva about a princess who ordered the world covered in leather so that she could walk the earth without soiling and hurting her feet. A wise counsel to her suggested that she cover her *feet* with leather instead—and thus shoes were invented.

Mindfulness practice is like the sole of the shoe. Mindfulness provides durable protection from the craggy and dangerous earth, yet does not expect the world to bow to the needs of the self.

The more you practice, the tougher and thicker this sole becomes. The more mindfulness is incorporated into daily life, the more protection you gain from its vicissitudes.

—ARNIE KOZAK,
Wild Chickens and Petty Tyrants

305

The practice of meditation invites us to investigate the flux of arising and passing events. When we get the hang of it, we can begin to see how each artifact of the mind is raised and lowered to view, like so many flashcards. But we can also glimpse, once in a while, the sleight-of-hand shuffling the cards and pulling them off the deck. Behind the objects lies a process. Self is a process. Self is a verb.

—ANDREW OLENDZKI,
Unlimiting Mind

306

From the inside, asking the meaning of life is like asking the meaning of a tree or the sky or the ocean. The meaning of a tree is to be tree; the meaning of the sky simply is the sky, and so on. We might say that from this perspective, the meaning of what's happening is inseparable from simply what's happening. And that "what" that's happening moment after moment is all the answer there is. In the end, our question isn't answered so much as it simply drops away.

—BARRY MAGID,
Ending the Pursuit of Happiness

307

Generating compassion does not mean actually freeing beings from their suffering; it is *wishing* that they be free. Of course, if there are things we can do to help, we should do them. Sometimes our efforts will work, sometimes not. The most skilled doctor is unable to cure every patient, and the most courageous rescue worker can't save every life. No matter how strongly we may wish someone to be free from a problem, we may not be able to bring this about. We can only try our best, and then accept whatever the result may be.

—KATHLEEN MCDONALD,
Awakening the Kind Heart

308

Every act can be one of offering and of encountering the Buddha. But I still have a special fondness for the incense offering and bow. Even if we are phony during the rest of the day, at that moment we are forced to confront who we are and how we are operating. If we are phony before the Buddha, we will be awakened to this fact. And if we are genuine before the Buddha, then our offering, bow, and *nembutsu* truly touches the heart of reality.

—JEFF WILSON,
Buddhism of the Heart

309

In the spiritual domain, our thought processes can act as filters or perceptual distortions that preclude us from realizing the deepest spiritual realities. When we cease believing that our mental overlays reflect the ultimate reality of life, we begin to experience the freedom that lies at the end of our journey. This is not freedom "from" something, but the freedom that comes from living without the self-constructed boundaries that limit our experience of peace, joy, and love.

—MATTHEW FLICKSTEIN,
The Meditator's Atlas

310

You can't awaken to something that isn't already present.

———

In an important way, enlightenment is simply being present in whatever one happens to be doing at the moment.

———

Our capacity for loving depends upon our being fully present.

—LIN JENSEN,
Deep Down Things

311

Being, or being present,
  cannot be an aim.
   Otherwise it's in the future.

If we were to cultivate this aim,
  we'd keep ourselves within
   the framework of becoming.

Being cannot be
  in the future or in the past.

We may speak of the present,
  of being, but being doesn't need
   any concept of time.

When we speak of the present
  it's to avoid slipping
   into past or future.

—CHARLES GENOUD,
Gesture of Awareness

312

All this struggling and striving to make the world better is a great mistake; not because it isn't a good thing to improve the world if you know how to do it, but because striving and struggling is the worst way you could set about doing anything.

—GEORGE BERNARD SHAW
IN *Joyously Through the Days*

313

Enlightenment understood as separable from the mind of compassion is not enlightenment. Insight without compassion would be little more than an unusual and intriguing turn of mind.

—SUSAN MURPHY,
Upside-Down Zen

314

Simple "letting go" cannot be achieved through our own efforts. Because, in those moments of feeling overwhelmed with a sense of powerlessness, we are powerless to even let go. We either cling desperately to what we have left or wallow in our debilitating and disturbing—yet somewhat snug and numb—inability to offer another hand to anybody or take another step forward.

We are tempted to settle into this snug, numb, cozy feeling, in a dazed state approaching suspended animation,

➥

unable to do anything for months or even years. It would make all the difference in the world if, before yielding to this temptation, we were to step back and take stock of ourselves. See what is happening to us. This is where Zen practice can be invaluable.

A moment of awareness of our utter powerlessness and no-thingness—when the only thing left "to do" is simply "to be" and admit it and accept it—can be the greatest turning point of our life. Simply "to be," shorn of all power "to do," places us at rock-bottom. At rock-bottom of what we are, there is no trace of self-construct to bank upon or cling to. There is only pure being, stripped of all "doing" and "having." In this state of total nakedness, what we are left with is simply "this very body"—breathing in, breathing out. Breathing in, breathing out.

—RUBEN L. F. HABITO,
Healing Breath

315

The mental function of faith is generally understood as being rooted in the emotional aspect of the human mind. However, the act of believing in Buddhism is not something limited to the realm of the emotions. Within the mental functions of faith there is actually the inclusion of all three human aspects of cognition, emotion, and volition, and thus the distinction of faith into these three aspects. Faith is a mental activity that mobilizes all elements possessed by human beings, to thrust us forward into a life based on truth.

—TAGAWA SHUN'EI,
Living Yogacara

316

My life seems inevitably to lead me to love what's been excluded, rejected, and unacknowledged, whether it's a woman's body or the Earth on which we have wrought so much havoc. It's become the path of reconciliation. The relationships I left out in my own life—with my body, the Earth's body, people of color—became precisely what I had to reconnect with and transform.

—CHINA GALLAND
IN *The Best of Inquiring Mind*

317

If you don't remember death, you don't remember the Dharma.

—LAMA ZOPA RINPOCHE,
How to Be Happy

318

This Mahamudra
Is not stained by any defilement;
It is neither to be negated nor affirmed;
It cannot be cultivated
Through the spiritual path and antidotes;
This perfect state of all the enlightened ones
Is the source of all excellent qualities
And spontaneous accomplishments.

—CHAKGYA CHENPO RABTU MINEYPAI GYU
IN *Mahamudra—The Moonlight*

319

The entire array of thought and nonthought,
appearances and no appearance, resting and no resting,
empty and not empty, clarity and no clarity,
are all one taste in the luminosity of the dharmakaya.

You see no appearances that are not the dharmakaya.
You see no thought that is not luminosity.

—LAMA SHANG

IN *Mahamudra and Related Instructions*

320

How should you meditate? You can sit if you want to sit, stand if you want to stand, work if you want to work, or busily take care of your daily life—all of these can be practicing meditation. Thus "sitting" meditation is possible in any circumstance—it is the mind that sits, not the body. As long as you let go and entrust with faith, your daily life itself can be meditation.

—DAEHAENG SUNIM,
No River to Cross

321

Though the difference between friends and enemies, between those who are right and those who are wrong, can feel very real, Buddhist analytical meditation always shows that such feelings, though temporally real, are ultimately illusory. Acting upon them leads to grief, regret, and suffering.

—RITA M. GROSS
IN *Mindful Politics*

322

No matter how deeply you concentrate, something is going to interrupt your beautiful, untrammeled emptiness.

The universe always comes back again. No matter how skillfully we meditate, emptiness won't stay empty for very long. Something always seems to keep popping up.

If your goal is to stay in Mu without breaks or interruptions, this oscillation will appear to pose an enormous problem. But if you stop assuming there's something wrong, you can sit back and enjoy the show, knowing it's the way things have to be. The oscillation is the natural order of things. In fact, it can't be stopped no matter what we do.

—KURT SPELLMEYER,
Buddha at the Apocalypse

323

The crucial factor influencing how well we can respond in any given situation seems to be the level of mindfulness we can bring to bear upon the moment. If we don't care to be present, unconscious decision-making systems will function by default to get us through to the next moment, albeit in the grips of (often flawed and suffering-causing) learned behaviors and conditioned responses. If, on the other hand, we can increase the amount of conscious awareness present by manifesting mindfulness, we expand the range of our possible responses. Even if disposed to anger, we can choose to act with kindness. This is the essence of our freedom in an otherwise heavily conditioned system.

—ANDREW OLENDZKI,
Unlimiting Mind

324

Since we experience sickness, why not experience sickness with the thought to benefit others?

Since we experience loss, why not experience loss with the thought to benefit others?

Since we experience hardships, why not experience hardships with the thought to benefit others?

Since we experience relationship problems, why not do so with the thought to benefit others?

Since we must experience death, why not experience even death with the thought to benefit others?

What life could be happier or more meaningful than this?

—LAMA ZOPA RINPOCHE,
How to Be Happy

325

When visiting a teacher or a center, examine the teacher's students. Are they simply clones-in-training of the teacher? This is probably not a good thing—after all, the Path is about becoming more fully yourself, not becoming more like your teacher. On the other hand, do the students seem to be people you like, and might like to be with? Can you recognize the values they advocate? Are they independent and engaged in the world? Can they joke about themselves? And, importantly, can they joke about their institution and teacher? And more important still: Do they seem to be genuinely on a path that is freeing them from their suffering?

This step of evaluating the community is an important one and one I strongly urge you not to skip. After all, the community, the sangha, is as much the teacher as the person with the title. Often, actually, the community is even more the teacher than the person with the title.

—JAMES ISHMAEL FORD,
Zen Master WHO?

326

Don't just follow what other people do; understand for yourself what the true path to freedom and happiness is, and then follow it. The decision you make is going to affect you, not just today, but in ten, twenty, or thirty years. Ask yourself: Are you prepared for old age, sickness, and death? This preparation has nothing to do with your material resources—such as finding a good nursing home—and everything to do with your spiritual resources. Are you able to let go of your health and realize it wasn't your health anyway—that it's just the nature of the body to be sick and weak? You need to learn how to die—how to die to the world, die to your possessions, die to all your hopes of material happiness. That is, you need to learn how to let go of everything. If you learn how to die early on in life, you're on the right track.

—AJAHN BRAHM,
The Art of Disappearing

327

Not being opposite anything—that is the samadhi of noncontention.

—GULIN

IN *Zen Under the Gun*

328

When meditation is used as a means of focusing on certain core teachings, it can facilitate a far less intellectually
driven relationship with ideas. The beliefs or concepts are
not argued, deconstructed, processed through affective
response, or passively accepted. Instead, there is a means
of *being with* such ideas/beliefs that is more experiential in
nature and offers a greater potential for transformation.

—PILAR JENNINGS,
Mixing Minds

329

I'm not striving for the ideal surfer's paradise anymore, or the perfect life without obstacles. It doesn't exist. Not that I don't have preferences or dreams. But it seems like the idea of paradise is just on the horizon, always, while life is *here*, under my feet, now.

Might as well enjoy it, learn to appreciate the good waves, the paddling, the ferocious storms, and the mundane moments—the quiet lulls between swells. Emptiness here, emptiness there, says one famous Zen poem, but the infinite universe stands always before your eyes; infinitely large and infinitely small.

—JAIMAL YOGIS,
Saltwater Buddha

330

If you believe your concepts are real, you will dwell confused.

—SHAILA CATHERINE,
Wisdom Wide and Deep

——

I must become skilled in knowing the ways of my own mind.

—*Anguttara Nikaya*
IN *Wisdom Wide and Deep*

331

From the world of passions,
returning to the world of passions.
There is a moment's pause—
if it rains, let it rain,
if the wind blows, let it blow.

—IKKYU
IN *Zen Radicals, Rebels, and Reformers*

332

I like to remember that the first noble truth—life is suffering—is the start of the path. Life is suffering, life is difficult, and it doesn't give us what we think we want and need. Suffering is what puts us on the path. Hindrance isn't a contradiction to the path, it is the path.

—JANE HIRSHFIELD
IN *Women Practicing Buddhism*

333

The Dharma tells us that while it's wonderful to be surrounded by congenial friends, they very rarely give us the opportunity to practice patience. What we need for that are people who will provoke, chafe, stir up, and aggravate. In our spirit of experimentation, only such people provide the opportunity to identify habitual negative patterns of thinking and replace them with more life-enhancing alternatives.

—

It's the way we experience something that matters more than the thing itself.

—DAVID MICHIE,
Enlightenment To Go

334

When you have developed powerful mindfulness, it's like going out into a beautiful garden in the brilliant sunshine. It's energizing and inspiring. Possessing strong mindfulness, such brightness of mind, if you then focus it on a small part of the world, you will see so deeply into its nature. The experience of bright and focused awareness is wonderful and amazing! You see much more beauty and truth than you ever imagined. Developing mindfulness is like turning up the lights of the mind.

—AJAHN BRAHM,
Mindfulness, Bliss, and Beyond

335

Births, deaths, graduations, marriages, and divorces are so plainly karmic ceremonies, marking the moments that shape the course of our lives. At each of these a "knot of karma," a knot of change that links birth to death, and links becoming to letting go, is tied forever. Then there are the "lesser" ceremonies of karma—of welcoming somebody into your house and sharing a meal or a cup of coffee with them, or going for a walk, or chopping the carrots, or kissing your child goodnight. Any action is lifted to ceremony by mindfulness. And ceremony, from the old Greek goddess Ceres, evokes reaping the entire rich harvest of the earth.

—SUSAN MURPHY,
Upside-Down Zen

336

The bodhisattva finds in prajna a sense of completion and is completely at peace with it and with herself. The prajna-wisdom is her support; through a deep understanding of the paradox of an ultimate lack of self-existence in things, she has the realization that there is nothing lacking anywhere. Whatever the limitations of her conditioned mind may be, she has a perfect understanding of, and trust in, the wisdom of shunyata. No deluded views cloud her vision.

—Mu Soeng,
The Heart of the Universe

337

In the Tibetan tradition, there is a practice known as "rejoicing." When we recognize good qualities in others such as compassion, kindness, wisdom, calmness, or strength, or when we see or hear of someone doing a positive, beneficial action such as giving, we rejoice: "How wonderful that is!" This is exactly what we aspire for when we generate loving-kindness, so it's only right to be joyful when people are doing what we wish them to do.

We also need to rejoice in our own positive actions and qualities. This is a very effective antidote to self-hatred and depression.

—KATHLEEN McDONALD,
Awakening the Kind Heart

338

Enlightened management is one way of taking religion seriously, profoundly, deeply, and earnestly.

—**ABRAHAM MASLOW**
IN *Business and the Buddha*

339

It is essential to urgently sit here, without a wall and without no-wall, appreciating and honoring those who came before us so that there may be those who come after us.

—**DOSHO PORT,**
Keep Me in Your Heart a While

340

Too much concern for success erodes our mind's flexibility and subtleness, and prevents us from appreciating life and its meaning.

———

Our inherent enlightenment is expressed when there are no strings attached to what we do.

—LES KAYE,
Joyously Through the Days

341

Be very attentive to the seductive illusions that can hide behind your spiritual interests and meditation practice. When something arouses you in a negative way or causes a reactive response, pay attention. Work against the impulse to project your response onto another person or onto the external situation. Don't just cover the disturbance and the response it elicits with a pious platitude or a spiritual slogan. Instead, cultivate the difficult habit of reflecting in your meditation on why you respond in that way. Ask yourself, "What afflictive mind state in me is being triggered here?"

———

Situations and other people are never as we think they are. Investigate rigorously and honestly the state of your own mind: that is the only place you can really make a difference.

—BOB SHARPLES,
Meditation and Relaxation in Plain English

342

The verse of contrition I was given to chant so many years ago has had consequences of its own. It has carried me beyond a simple "I'm sorry" to an appreciation of the circumstances in which we all live, the ways in which we try and fail, and try and fail again. I'm a partner now in the brotherhood and sisterhood of inevitable error and recovery.

———

If I have a chance at the time of my death to take an accounting of what I've done, I won't be asking how enlightened I've become, I'll be asking how much I've shown kindness to others.

—LIN JENSEN,
Together Under One Roof

343

I cultivated depth of mind for one hundred timeless eons. Because of that I became free from being an ordinary person and attained unsurpassable complete enlightenment. I call myself Vairochana and reside in the ocean of the lotus blossom pedestal. There are one thousand petals around this pedestal. Each petal is one world, which becomes one thousand worlds. I take the form of a thousand Shakyamunis and am based in the thousand worlds. Then within the world of one petal there are also one billion Mount Sumerus as well as so many suns and moons, heavens and earths, Jambudvipa continents, and Bodhisattva Shakyamunis who sit under a billion bodhi trees and expound the bodhisattvas' depth of mind.

—*Indra's Net Sutra*
IN *Lotus*

344

Our training is not about doing something difficult to become something special. Chanting sutras, doing prostrations, working, we receive this very moment, and for that we have eternal gratitude. In every single thing we do, we find Buddha. In knowing that we are alive today, we find our greatest grace and joy.

—

The true liberation of all beings can happen only when we are without any idea of helping at all. When we go into the world with that state of mind, for the first time we can truly function. This is what is most necessary in society today. When we function without force or attachment in our relations, we have the power to bring forth each other's deepest state of mind.

—SHODO HARADA,
Moon by the Window

345

The power of self-expression to both help and harm is the focus of the discipline of right speech. This power is contained not just in the semantic contents of words but also in the use of silence, gesture, facial expression, timing, and the more subtle implications of the context and emotional tone in which words are spoken. These more subtle aspects of the art of self-expression often reveal core understandings and intentions as much as, if not more than, words themselves.

—RISHI SATIVIHARI,
Unlearning the Basics

346

Every thought, emotion, intention, attitude, or aspiration is shaping how ensuing experience will unfold. This means that every single moment of consciousness is a moment of practice, whether we like it or not. We are practicing to become ourselves. The important question is really just how much we want to participate in the process.

—

The reason we put so much time and care and effort into learning, through meditation, how to be with whatever is arising in experience without greed, hatred, or delusion is because by suspending their influence upon us in this moment, we become free of their effects in the next moment. How we hold ourselves *right now* is the key to everything we will become. It is that important.

—Andrew Olendzki,
Unlimiting Mind

347

We see multiple cause-effect relationships in our choices, understanding how they condition future options and situations. We realize that each choice to indulge a habit, obsession, compulsion, or addiction tilts the balance, making it easier to so choose the next time. We see how each "no" to unwholesomeness makes saying "no" again easier. We realize that nothing is free; everything counts and has its consequences.

—MARY JO MEADOW,
Christian Insight Meditation

348

If people are to teach this sutra,
Let them enter the Tathagata's room,
Put on the Tathagata's robe,
And sit on the Tathagata's seat.

Facing the multitude without fear,
Let them teach it clearly everywhere,
With great compassion as their room,

Gentleness and patience as their robe,
And the emptiness of all things as their seat.
Doing this, they should teach the Dharma.

—BUDDHA
IN *The Lotus Sutra*

349

I spoke with teacher of mine about fierce compassion. She asked me if I knew how Durga defeated the demons. Yes, I told her: Durga pierced the heart of the king of the demons with her dagger. She said, "Yes, piercing the heart is opening the heart." Then I understood the story. Only by opening the heart can the world be saved, one more time.

—CHINA GALLAND
IN *The Best of Inquiring Mind*

350

Karma is the observation that everything has causes and everything has consequences; rebirth is the observation that I am constantly being created and recreated by each succeeding moment.

—JAMES ISHMAEL FORD,
If You're Lucky, Your Heart Will Break

351

Generally, we think of enlightenment as something that happens all at once, like a tidal wave that cleans everything impure away. However, this is not actually how realization happens. Realization happens *incrementally*, from moment to moment.

—DEBORAH SCHOEBERLEIN,
Mindful Teaching and Teaching Mindfulness

352

When life is fair and sunlight gilds the day
When fortune smiles and flowers adorn our way;
Oft let us pause with grateful hearts to say
Namu Amida Butsu.

E'en though our way leads 'neath a darkened sky
And to our loved one pain and death draw nigh;
Our tears may flow, yet trustingly we cry
Namu Amida Butsu.

—PURE LAND BUDDHIST SONG
IN *Heaven and Earth Are Flowers*

353

It occurs to me that the *who* of "Who am I?" might not be the best interrogative pronoun for the inquiry. "Where am I?" might serve better.

—LIN JENSEN,
Deep Down Things

354

Bitterness held with integrity and humor turns out in the fullness of time to have a quality of ineffable sweetness that nourishes everyone who comes in contact with it; the bitter is transformed into life-bestowing bitt-*Ahh*-ness. White combs of sweetest honey, formed entirely in the dark.

—SUSAN MURPHY,
Upside-Down Zen

355

Every part of every day is an open invitation for quiet reflection and mindful awareness. We can do this in our prison cell, on the bus, during coffee break at work, in front of a pile of dishes, while walking from here to there. Each fork in the road is another chance not to give in to set patterns and old habits. It is the perfect time to take the path that allows our attention to turn within and experience the freedom we all seek.

—CALVIN MALONE,
Razor-Wire Dharma

356

We don't have to buy everything the mind tries to sell us just because the salesperson is between our ears.

—ARNIE KOZAK,
Wild Chickens and Petty Tyrants

357

As soon as nonduality is realized,
even though suffering is not yet eliminated
and the power of the qualities are not developed,
who can say that this isn't the path of seeing?

When the sun rises in the morning,
it does not immediately melt the ice
and the ground and stones stay cold,
but who can deny that it's the sun?

—LAMA SHANG

IN *Mahamudra and Related Instructions*

358

Standing on the firm ground of facts, Buddhism welcomes all progress and has never contested the prerogative of reason to be the ultimate truth, and, accordingly, requires nothing to be accepted without inquiry. Reason, says Buddhism, not superstition, not mere tradition, not the will to believe, not pragmatic utility, must be the foundation.

Zen aims at nothing but this reason. You are, however, not allowed to speak this reason, or to think of this reason, but to live in it as the fish, without knowing it, lives in the water.

—Nyogen Senzaki,
Eloquent Silence

359

When you look at a river, think that just as the river
flows, life finishes just as quickly.
As the sun rises and sets, reflect that life passes
just as quickly.
As the oil in a burning lamp is steadily consumed,
so too is your life.
As the seasons pass, so does your life; as summer,
autumn, winter, and spring pass quickly by,
so does your life, becoming shorter and shorter,
finishing more and more quickly.

This kind of practice is useful because it prevents your
mind from becoming deluded; it makes your mind aware
of change, of life becoming shorter, of the brevity of human
life, of this precious human life.

—LAMA ZOPA RINPOCHE,
Wholesome Fear

360

If we understand the momentary nature of realization, then each moment becomes a great opportunity for us. It is the opportunity for practice, for realization. Each moment is precious, because we have the opportunity to start fresh and to see, nakedly, the dharmakaya once again and experience a moment of enlightenment.

—ANYEN RINPOCHE,
Momentary Buddhahood

361

When we can fully see our own time in the dynamic fullness of all time, without being blind to cause and effect, without being caught by limiting views of time itself, we can begin to be the present time in the depths of time, to presence the deep time that includes and honors the presence right now of our ancestors.

—TAIGEN DAN LEIGHTON,
Zen Questions

362

Whatever form it takes, practice is a call to pay attention to who we think we are, what kind of questions we are asking, what form we expect an answer to take, and what are our curative fantasies of what will happen once we find the answer.

—BARRY MAGID,
Ending the Pursuit of Happiness

363

Do we need a Story of Everything, to identify with and place ourselves within? The Buddha told a parable about a foolish man shot by a poisoned arrow, who insists on learning who shot the arrow, what his caste is, what the arrow is made of, and so forth, before he will allow anyone to pull it out.

The Dharma is a raft for ferrying across the river of samsara, not a Big Story to be carried on our backs everywhere we go.

—DAVID R. LOY,
The World Is Made of Stories

364

Flowers as they are
in the lotus pond:
My offering to the spirits.

—BASHO MATSUO

IN *Lotus*

365

"So that's it," she said, not looking up. "That's what it comes down to: nothing makes me happy."

"Yeah," he said. "It makes me happy too."

—DEAN SLUYTER
IN *You Are Not Here*

Supplements

1: Developing Compassion for an Antagonist

by Lama Zopa Rinpoche,
in *How to Be Happy*

How can you develop compassion for someone who hates you?

First of all, you have to see that the person is completely overwhelmed by ignorance, anger, and the dissatisfied mind of desire. It is important to immediately recall that the person has no freedom at all but is completely overwhelmed, almost possessed, by delusions—just as Tibet was overwhelmed and possessed by the Chinese. The person who hates you is surely overwhelmed by not just one delusion but many.

Rather than thinking that the person is the *same* as their anger, is *one with* their anger—which is not the reality—you have to see that the person and their delusion, their anger, are separate. Even if the person hallucinates they are one with their anger, they are not. What's more, thinking that they are one with their anger—rather than sufferingly afflicted by it themselves—will only make you more upset. Whereas if you think that the person and their anger are different, as they are indeed different in reality, then there is some space in your mind for compassion to arise.

347

Even if this person who hates you experiences pleasure in hating you, their pleasure is really suffering that is just appearing as pleasure. The person who hates you may call their hatred "pleasure," but it is still only suffering. It is just a question of whether the person notices that. This is the second reason why the person who hates you is an object of compassion.

The third reason is that he or she, just like you, also experiences "the suffering of suffering"—which means rebirth, old age, sickness, death, meeting undesirable objects, separating from desirable ones, and all the other countless problems of life. How painful for that person!

On top of all these sufferings, out of delusion the person who hates you creates the karma to suffer *yet more*—to be born yet again into the suffering realms.

And then, if you do not practice patience in response to that anger, do not cultivate compassion for this suffering being, and instead return anger to that person, by requiting that anger, you are pushing that suffering being toward *still more* harming karma. You are throwing him or her over the precipice into the unimaginable suffering of the lower realms.

When you reflect on all this, there is no real choice: you have to feel compassion for each person—even for the one who appears to you as an enemy!

2: Unusual Experiences During Meditation

by B. Alan Wallace,
in *The Attention Revolution*

The Vajra Essence *emphasizes above all that there is no consistency in the specific experiences from one individual to the next. Everyone's mind is so unimaginably complex that there is no way to predict with confidence the types of experiences each person will experience. Here is a list of just some of the kinds of meditative experiences that may arise during this training, especially when it is pursued in solitude for many hours each day, for months on end:*

The impression that all your thoughts are wreaking havoc in your body and mind, like boulders rolling down a steep mountain, crushing and destroying everything in their path

A sharp pain in your heart as a result of all your thoughts, as if you had been pierced with the tip of a sword

The ecstatic, blissful sense that mental stillness is pleasurable, but movement is painful

The perception of all phenomena as brilliant, colored particles

349

Intolerable pain throughout your body from the tips of the
hair on your head down to the tips of your toenails

The sense that even food and drink are harmful due to your
being afflicted by a variety of physical disorders

An inexplicable sense of paranoia about meeting other people, visiting their homes, or being in public places

Compulsive hope in medical treatment, divinations, and
astrology

Such unbearable misery that you think your heart will burst

Insomnia at night, or fitful sleep like that of someone who
is critically ill

Grief and disorientation when you wake up

The conviction that there is still some decisive understanding or knowledge that you must have, and yearning for it
like a thirsty person longing for water

The emergence, one after another, of all kinds of afflictive
thoughts, and being impelled to pursue them, as painful
as that may be

Various speech impediments and respiratory ailments

The conviction that there is some special meaning in every
external sound that you hear and form that you see, and
thinking, "That must be a sign or omen for me," compul-
sively speculating about the chirping of birds and everything else you see and feel

The sensation of external sounds and voices of humans,
dogs, birds, and so on all piercing your heart like thorns

Unbearable anger due to the paranoia of thinking that everyone else is gossiping about you and putting you down

Negative reactions when you hear and see others joking around and laughing, thinking that they are making fun of you, and retaliating verbally

Because of your own experience of suffering, compulsive longing for others' happiness when you watch them

Fear and terror about weapons and even your own friends because your mind is filled with a constant stream of anxieties

Everything around you leading to all kinds of hopes and fears

When you get into bed at night, premonitions of others who will come the next day

Uncontrollable fear, anger, obsessive attachment, and hatred when images arise, seeing others' faces, forms, minds, and conversations, as well as demons and so forth, preventing you from falling asleep

Weeping out of reverence and devotion to your gurus, your faith and devotion in the objects of religious devotion, your sense of renunciation and disillusionment with the cycle of existence, and your heartfelt compassion for sentient beings

Rough experiences, followed by the disappearance of all your suffering and the saturation of your mind with radiant clarity and ecstasy, like pristine space

The experience that gods or demons are actually carrying away your head, limbs, and vital organs, leaving behind only a vapor trail; or merely having the sensation of this happening, or it occurring in a dream

A sense of ecstasy as if a stormy sky had become free of
   clouds

While many of us would likely respond to some of those
disagreeable experiences by stopping the practice or seeking medical help, Dudjom Lingpa actually called them all
"signs of progress"! It truly is progress when you recognize
how cluttered and turbulent your mind is. But the deeper
you venture into the inner wilderness of the mind, the more
you encounter all kinds of unexpected and, at times, deeply
troubling memories and impulses that manifest both psy-
chologically and physically. At times, these may become so
disturbing that psychological counseling or medical treatment may be necessary. Dudjom Lingpa's advice is to stay a
steady course in the practice, continuing to observe whatever comes up, without distraction and without grasping.
This is a tall order, but it is the way forward. There is no
way to probe the depths of consciousness except by way of
the psyche, with all its neuroses and imbalances. It should
come as some solace that none of these unnerving experiences are freshly introduced into your mind by meditative
practice. Whatever comes up was already there, previously
hidden by the turbulence and dullness of the mind.

3: Post–Meditation Practices

by Ethan Nichtern,
in *One City*

Here are the three post-meditation practices that I try to remember every day.

(1) I try to question one consumption choice that I make every day. If I can refrain from consuming the chosen item, then I try to offer the money to a person or cause who needs it. If I don't refrain, I at least try to find a way to consume it that causes less suffering and more benefit in the network of interdependence. For instance, take one item of food you eat each day and see if it can be found locally and organically. This daily mindful consumption practice has led to a much greater curiosity about the structures of my consumption choices, as well as greater curiosity into the ethics of companies that I support financially.

(2) I pick up and dispose of three pieces of garbage that I did not create each time I go outside. Of course, this doesn't make NYC much cleaner. But it does cause me to slow down for a moment, to become aware of my concrete surroundings, and to apply mindfulness to a specific task. Most importantly, it gives me the

opportunity to engage with the awkward emotions that arise in my mind from having to bend over and pick up a candy wrapper in front of others on a crowded street. This practice adds about four seconds to my commute.

(3) I try to say "thank you" every time a service is performed for me, every time I am part of a financial transaction. This cuts through any sense of entitlement, that money means I somehow own the people who serve me, reminding me that money is solely an abstraction of shared human energy that allows our interdependent needs to be met.

Three is a good number of practices. They should be short and simple, requiring the application of mindfulness in the present moment and awareness of your mind's role in your environment. Come up with your own list of three simple daily practices and do them for two weeks. At the end, you can renew or alter the practices.

4: "Secret Practices"

by Barry Magid,
in *Ending the Pursuit of Happiness*

When we think we're just sitting, just paying attention to the moment, nonetheless there are all sorts of ways in which we are subtly shaping our experience into some background narrative or explanation. We can go on for a long time, thinking that we're "just sitting," and still really never dig down into those underlying core beliefs. Traditional Zen practice can all too easily use the cover of "just sitting" to collude with an unexamined personal "secret practice" grounded in curative fantasy and emotional dissociation. What looks on the surface like a direct or simple engagement with the moment can all too easily fall into a complacent avoidance of our underlying emotional issues.

We may all fall into that complacency in our sitting from time to time, but if we're honest, life is continually offering us reminders to wake up and go deeper. What are those reminders? Anger, anxiety, restlessness, boredom—just to name a few. Each one of these is reminding us that in some way life isn't conforming to one of our underlying expectations. And that's where we have to dig. Anger marks the spot! We have to dig down and find a way to make consciously explicit to ourselves those vague, half-formulated ways of shaping experience that are rubbing up against some inconvenient bit of reality and setting off that emotional reaction. Once we can make them explicit, they become simply one more thought that we can become aware of as it passes through our consciousness. *That old story again.* But until we're really clear and familiar with those old patterns, they'll work busily and continuously in the background, especially during those times when we think we're just sitting, doing nothing.

Real sitting isn't a passive, low-energy drift through the zazen period. Sitting must be alert, active, aware. We should constantly have our antennae out to pick up every sight and sound and feeling that arises in our body. And we have to make that level of attention second nature, like a frog who seems to sit dreamily on his lily pad, but as soon as a fly goes by—ZAP! He wasn't sitting so passively after all.

So: Just sit. Leave everything alone. Do nothing. But really do it.

5: Moving Meditation

by Charles Genoud, in _Gesture of Awareness_

There are professional meditators
    who can sit quietly for hours, but now
    I'm disturbing everything.

Can you remove
    the meditation cushion?

> _you may walk_
>
> _just be walking_
>
> _can you be_
> _at two places at_
> _the same time_
>
> _you may try_
>
> _be at two places at_
> _the same time_
>
> _you may walk_
> _slowly or_
> _fast_
>
> _but be at two places_
> _at the same time_

if you can't

then be
every instant
in one place

you may stop

you may let your eyes close and
just be
standing

experiencing

nothing to change

nothing to improve

can we feel the floor
beneath our feet

feel its
temperature

feel its
texture

is it hard or
soft

cold

warm

can we just be
standing

without interfering

without changing anything

without keeping anything

feeling how heavy
or light
you are

can I be

can I stand

as a way
of being

a simple way
of being

you may walk

and stop

and see

where has your walking
gone

you may walk

where has your standing
gone

you may move

and stop

and know

where has your moving
gone

can we be moving and
standing still
at the same time

you may try

explore

moving

stopping
moving
at the same time

you may stop

close your eyes

can you slightly
lift
your shoulders

slightly

maybe an inch
or so

and feel
what is happening
within yourself

being open or
not to what
is happening

respect what you feel

slowly let them
come down

feel the way
the shoulders
come down

we're not interested
in having shoulders
down or up

but rather

in the movement
of life that
manifests

while moving our shoulders
down or up

can you lift
your shoulders

you can leave them up

and feel what's happening
within yourself

slowly let them
down

standing

open your eyes

and just walk as a way
of being

not
going
anywhere

6: Working on a Koan with a Teacher

by Susan Murphy, in *Upside-Down Zen*

Working on a koan closely with a teacher may require you to call up the whole great world in all its minute particularities, right there in the interview room with an abundant economy of means. The whole world is there at your disposal, so you just use it. Here it is! A tree, a buffalo, a stone from the bottom of the sea. It's also like play in that it has absolutely no purpose and makes no utilitarian sense. This is the great guarantee of a koan: it will not make sense; it will not be amenable to our usual paths of making sense. It is a little like a ball game, demanding direct throwing and catching. A koan is not a thing that you can mull over and maul and masticate. There's nothing worse than an overmasticated koan. If you cannot respond freely from your own being, it is better to remain silent and sit some more with the koan.

A koan has that directness because it is coming from stillness; it is nothing other than that vast alive stillness. If you think about an accomplished athlete or actor, there's a great quality in them of the stillness that is learned from play. It's play that teaches us so well about profound stillness. Practice, or koan work, is a game that does not involve so much moves of the mind as radical removes of the mind.

It involves taking away elements that we've grown to rely on. Again, this is like play, like games, like play-acting of a certain kind. Just getting down to a bare stage and very little to rely on; in fact, nothing at all.

7: SELECTIONS FROM
The Ultimate Supreme Path of Mahamudra

**by Lama Shang (1123–93),
in *Mahamudra and Related Instructions***

The View

Whether the conquerors of the three times appear or
    don't appear,
whether the aryas realize it or don't realize it,
whether the buddhas teach it or don't teach it,
whether the commentators explain it or don't explain it,
this pure, elaboration-free luminosity of the true nature
is primordially, naturally present, with neither increase nor
    decrease.

Worlds are formed within pure space and are destroyed
by burning fire, scattering winds, and so on.
Although this destruction occurs throughout many incal-
    culable eons,
space remains unharmed, never altered, and neither
    increases nor decreases.

There is darkness when the sun's primordial brightness
is completely obscured by clouds, and there is brightness
    when the clouds vanish.

Despite this apparent increase and decrease,
it is impossible for the sun's essence to increase or decrease.

The unchanging dharmakaya, which is present in the
     same way,
is nothing other than your own mind.
The entire variety of samsara and nirvana arise in the mind.
The sufferings of the world and its beings arise from the
     confusion
caused by the erroneous delusion of not understanding
     your own mind.

When you have definite understanding of your own mind,
there will be great bliss and the infinite wisdom of nirvana.
Everything manifests from your own mind.
When you recognize the true nature of your mind,
you will know the true nature of all beings.
Knowing that, you will know nirvana and all other
     phenomena.
Knowing all phenomena, you will transcend all three realms.
By knowing one thing, you become wise in all.
By pulling up the roots, the leaves and petals naturally
     wither.
Therefore, gain certainty in the mind alone.

This true nature of the mind, the seed of everything,
primordially identical with the minds of all conquerors and
     their children,
is present as the birthless dharmakaya.

It is immaterial, self-knowing, and self-illuminating.
It is not a thing: It has no color, shape, or size.
It isn't nothing: Through conditions, it appears
    as everything.
It isn't permanent: It is empty by nature.
It isn't nonexistent: Its nature is unchanging self-illumination.
It is not a self: When examined, it has no essence.
It is not selfless: It is the great selfhood of freedom from
    elaboration.
It is not the extremes: It has no fixation whatsoever.
It is not the middle way: It is devoid of all dependency.
It cannot be identified by an example's names and symbols.
It has no example: It is like space.
It is not words: It cannot be described by speech.
It is not wordless: It is the cause of all expressions.

It cannot be reached through words such as
existence and nonexistence, truth and falsity,
empty and not empty, peace and no peace,
elaborated and unelaborated,
conceivable and inconceivable,
happiness and suffering, perceivable and unperceivable,
dual and nondual, beyond the intellect and not beyond the
    intellect,
devoid and not devoid, existent and nonexistent,
pure and impure, naturally present and not naturally present.

However profound the words used are,
and however many synonyms are employed,
it is impossible for them to pinpoint the true nature of
    the mind.

However wise you are, however profound your analysis,
though you describe it for many incalculable eons,
it will be impossible to realize the true nature of the mind,
for its natural condition is not an object for analysis.

However well you try to sieve for
the planets and stars that appear in a lake,
it is impossible to catch a single planet or star,
because those planets and stars are not existent things.

However long you use words to describe it,
no matter what refined terms you use, they are not the
    true nature.
For however long you analyze with your mind,
no matter how profound your understanding, that is not
    the true nature.

As long as there is the duality of seer and seen,
it is impossible to realize the nondual true nature.

In brief, to think that things "are" is the root of attachment
    to everything.
From the root of attachment all samsara develops.

If you identify by thinking "It's emptiness,"
or thinking "It is signless and aspirationless,"
thinking "It is unidentifiable," thinking "It is completely
    pure,"
thinking "It is birthless," thinking "It is unperceivable,"

thinking "It has no nature," thinking "It is without
     elaboration,"
thinking "It is not an object for analysis by speech or mind,"
thinking "It is uncreated and naturally present," and so on,
however profound these thoughts, our recognition of
     emptiness
will not transcend the conceptualization of an arrogant
     mind.
Attachment to concepts leads to a fall into inferior states
and a continuous ripening of karma from inferior actions.

If the chronic condition of samsara is not cured, the illness
     will continue to occur.
Meditators who have views created by their intellect
remain chronically ill from attachment to sectarianism.
You must have the innate knowledge that is free of
     thought.

It's impossible that even Shakyamuni could see what is
     described by
"There are embellishments that are provisional in meaning,
while this is the definitive meaning, the true nature."
Even what I'm saying now cannot fathom it.
Understand that it's like a finger pointing at the moon.

If you understand this, words and terminology will not
     obscure;
you will be unstained by the faults of words.
Therefore, without abandoning words and analysis,
have no arrogant attachment to their meaning.

The true nature of your own mind
pervades all beings, including their afflictions,
thoughts, aggregates, sensory elements and bases,
and all worlds, including their earth, stones, plants, and
    trees.

In brief, it pervades everything without exception,
including all inner and outer things.
That pervasion is without the duality of pervader and
    pervaded;
it is the manifestation of one single great identity.

All the planets and stars that appear on a lake
are pervaded by the lake, from which they cannot be
    separated.
All the waves that move upon the water
are pervaded by water and are inseparable from it.

The movement of mirages in the air
are pervaded by the air and are inseparable from it.

Statues, jewelry, and so on, which are made of gold,
are pervaded by gold and are inseparable from it.

Representations of the six kinds of beings made from
    molasses
are pervaded by molasses and are inseparable from it.
Space is not separate from a rainbow;
a rainbow is nothing other than space.
The rainbow is space, and space is the rainbow.
They are not separate; they are inseparable and indivisible.

In the same way, the mind and the variety of appearances
     are inseparable.
The mind and emptiness are inseparable;
emptiness and bliss are a great inseparability, a sameness.
In the same way, existence and nirvana are inseparable.

This pervading mind is the mahamudra.
Its nature is empty, so there is nothing to be identified.
Its characteristic is clarity—[the mind's] cognition can
     manifest anything.
Its essence is their inseparability, the union of the vajra mind.
The precious mind is the source of countless qualities.
It is inexhaustible, imperishable, indestructible,
and no one can steal it, this mind that is the treasury of
     space,
the mind that is as pure as crystal, untarnished by stains.

The mind is like a lamp's flame: It is self-knowing and
     self-illuminating.
The mind has the essence of enlightenment: It has a nature
     of luminosity.
The mind is like a river: It is a constant continuum.
The mind is like space: There is nothing that can be
     identified.

It is a mind of immaterial wisdom, completely transparent,
like a clean vessel filled with water.

The mind, from which arises all appearances that result
     from propensities,
is like the surface of a polished and unblemished mirror.

Forsaking Activities

However wise you are in contemplating and analyzing
    words,
if you do not practice, nothing will arise from within.
It's impossible for intellect's conceptual labeling to realize
    the true nature.
If you do not realize the true nature, it is impossible to
    purify your propensities.
Therefore, do not be attached to the academic wisdom of
    words,
but practice the instructions from the guru.

Repeating like a parrot becomes a song of aging and death.
Blind to yourself and others, there is the danger of falling
    into an abyss.

When you are practicing the sacred instructions,
have no attachment to life or body and forsake activities.
Even if you are hungry, cold, sick, or dying from starvation,
forsake everything, for they are just a dream.

Even if everyone reviles you and you acquire a bad
    reputation,
be humble and dedicate yourself to the essence of
    practice.

The fear of death from cold and hunger
is a cause for not abandoning worldly activities.
The few qualities that this beggar monk Shang has
are the benefit of using my life and body like targets.

Even if you have abandoned all wealth, right down to a
    needle and thread,
if you worry about supporting yourself, you are not a
    renunciate.
If you don't reject the wish to avoid what is bad,
there will never be a time when you abandon worldly
    activities.

If you do not banish the entire world from your mind,
even though you can be generous, maintain conduct,
make offerings to the guru, remain in solitude,
dedicate yourself to meditation, have good experiences,
have great wisdom, have high realization,
or perform any good action, you will just be meaninglessly
    tiring yourself.

If you don't understand how to banish the world from
    your mind
and you don't even wish for the happiness of the devas,
it's obvious that you must be aspiring for happiness in
    this life.

As long as thoughts have not ceased,
it's impossible to avoid preoccupation with future days.
Therefore, cast everything aside, become a devotee of the
    sacred.
Devote yourself to the treasury of instructions,
be unaffected by the armies of outer and inner maras,
and maintain a pure conduct whether in public or in
    private.

If you can do this by yourself, then wander alone in the
    mountains.
Maintain a pure conduct, free of pretense.
Have a motivation to benefit others, free of bias and
    attachment.
Develop the aspiration for enlightenment for the sake of all
    beings.
Apply yourself to genuine practice that is neither too tight
    nor too loose.

Practice the instructions just as they have been taught,
without focusing the mind on any happiness or
    unhappiness,
such as danger to life, heat and cold, hunger and thirst,
and without becoming seduced by fame and material
    wealth.

The Method of Meditation

A guru who has the quintessence of realization
directly introduces them to the wisdom they already have,
as if it were a treasure in their own hands.
They should remain, without distraction, in a state of
    nonmeditation,
where there is neither meditator nor anything on which to
    meditate.

The desire for numerous complexities
obscures the naturally present wisdom.
There is no need for a precise plan of action
in the meditation of mahamudra;
it does not have the stages of preliminaries, a main part,

and a conclusion, nor does it have any definitive numbers;
there is no need to calculate times and dates.
Whenever one has mindfulness, rest with relaxation.

Your mind is birthless and continuous,
without a beginning, middle, or end.

The rising and sinking of agitated waves
ceases by itself without interference.
This mind that is obscured by thoughts,
when left as it is, unmodified, will clarify as the
    dharmakaya.

Do not modify it, but rest in relaxation.
Do not control the mind, but let it go free.
Do not have intentions, but be spacious.
Do not focus on anything, but be expansive.

Do not be overactive, but rest in stillness.
Do not seek out somewhere to rest the mind;
rest without any basis, like space.

Keep the mind fresh, without thinking
of the past, the future, or the present.

Whether thoughts are appearing or not,
do not purposefully meditate, but rest naturally.

In brief, do not meditate on anything,
but let the mind go wherever it wants.

There is no need to be afraid of anything:
You will never depart from the dharmakaya.
Just by allowing the mind to relax
there will be an experience of clarity and nonthought,
and you will rest as if in the center of pure space:
This is the luminosity, the dharmakaya.

When a thought instantly springs from
that resting state,
do not think of it as something that is
other than the luminosity, the dharmakaya.

It is the same as when waves rise
from a clear, still sea
and are nothing other
than that clear sea.

The mind is the basis of thoughts.
Clarity and knowing are the characteristics of the mind.
Emptiness is the nature of that clarity and knowing.
Great bliss is the essence of emptiness.

The darkness of concepts has never existed
within the nature of the mind,
and so it is named *luminosity*.
Its knowing and emptiness are inseparable,
And therefore it is named union.

The nature of all phenomena
is the essence of the mind's knowing.
The essence of the mind's knowing

has no body with features;
it is a bodiless body, which is the supreme body.

Bodilessness is the body of the "true nature" (*dharmata*),
and therefore it is named the "truth body" (dharmakaya).

Therefore, the appearance of a thought
is emptiness appearing from emptiness,
the dharmakaya appearing from the dharmakaya,
luminosity appearing from luminosity,
union appearing from union,
the dharmadhatu appearing from the dharmadhatu,
purity appearing from purity,
Vajrasattva appearing from Vajrasattva,
enlightenment appearing from enlightenment.

Ignorant persons, who have no propensities from previous
    training
and have not obtained the true instructions,
make a distinction between the appearance
and the nonappearance of thoughts,
between thought and nonthought,
and between the mind and the dharmakaya.

They see thoughts as faults and stop them.
They wish for nonthought and deliberately create it,
but the wandering waves keep on moving.

The nonthought created by stopping thought
is thought. It is a delusion.
It is a great darkness that obscures the dharmakaya.

Those who do not wish to give rise to thought
are those who wish to remain in nonthought.
That desire leads to becoming a *gongpo* demon
and exhausts the treasury of natural wealth.
Meditators who stop their thoughts
are like people churning water for butter:
They will not see any benefit, even if they meditate for an eon.

Therefore, it's unnecessary to stop thoughts.
If they've stopped, there is no need to create them.
Though they appear, the dharmakaya is also present,
for they do not depart from the dharmakaya.

If you have the instructions from a sublime guru,
when there is movement, there is liberation; and when
     there is stillness, there is liberation.
Without instructions from a sublime guru,
when there is movement, there is bondage; and when
     there is stillness, there is bondage.

Therefore, you must receive the instructions.
Be certain that thoughts arise as your friends.
Refrain from preoccupying yourself with much analysis.
Instead, relax freely and be naturally at rest.

Do not follow after externals,
but let the mind go wherever it wants.

Do not look at external objects.
Do not even look at your own mind.

The objects are empty and the mind too is empty.
There is no need to feel afraid.

If you think, "This is it,"
that will plant the seed of attachment to an object.
If the seedling of conceit appears,
it will grow into the tree of samsara.

Do not obscure the mind with the darkness of
    meditation,
for the mind is primordially pure and luminous,
and meditation will destroy the effortless result.

Do not stir up the turbidity of desire
in the clear sea of the mind,
for that will obscure the jewels of the dharmakaya.

Do not smear the stains of meditation
upon the unblemished mirror of the mind,
for then you will not see the reflection of wisdom.

Do not use the clay of concepts to cover up
the precious jewel of the mind,
for that will prevent the desired and required result.

In brief, rest the mind without thinking, "This is it!"
Rest the mind without thinking, "This isn't it!"
The mind's thoughts of "is" and the mind's thoughts of
    "isn't"
are two mutually dependent fixations.

If there is absolutely no "is" at all,
then there will be absolutely no "isn't" at all.

Let go completely in a state free from thinking.
Don't think of "resting" or "not resting."
Don't think of "letting go" or "not letting go."
Don't even think "Think!" or "Don't think!"

Whether you are moving, sitting, or standing,
whether you are meditating, sleeping, or eating,
whether you are talking, sleeping, or anything,
it's essential that it be done with the natural mind.

Experience

Rest your own mind, this naturally present dharmakaya,
as it is, without modification,
and specific experiences will happen.

There are three kinds: those of the gradualist,
the indeterminate, and the immediate.

The way that experiences happen for gradualists:
At first there is simply resting,
then experiences definitely happen,
and then clear realization arises.

When there is the first state of resting,
thoughts arise uninterruptedly,
like water rushing down a cliff.
So you think, "Am I not able to meditate?"

The experience of this amount of thoughts arising
is the result of the mind being able to rest a little.
Before you rested in this way,
thoughts arose as they wished,
and you were not aware of the procession of thoughts.

Next, the mind slows and thoughts diminish,
becoming like a slowly moving river.

Then the mind will rest, immovable and stable,
like the depths of the ocean.

Then there will come experiences:
experiences of clarity, nonthought, and bliss,
like the center of pure space.
There is undistracted self-illumination,
like a lamp's flame undisturbed by wind.
There is lucidity, vividness, and ease,
like a rainfall of beautiful flowers.
There is brightness, evenness, and insubstantiality,
like the sun shining in a cloudless sky.
There is transparency and purity,
like a bronze vessel filled with water.

There is no end to words such as these.
They have no basis, appearing like dreams.
They are insubstantial, appearing like rainbows.
They are ungraspable, appearing like the moon on water.
It is like enjoying the pleasures of space—
everything is experienced but is experienced as nothing.

This nonexperience is the supreme experience.
All experiences have gone away.
Within nonexperience, there is nothing to be freed from.

Nondual Realization
When you have those kinds of experiences,
realization's wisdom clearly arises.
If realization's wisdom doesn't arise,
however excellent those experiences may be,
they're like cutting down a tree but not touching the roots,
so that the agony of the afflictions will still grow.

Therefore, the arising of realization is crucial.
The arising of the wisdom of realization
certainly does not happen through desire,
it does not come through skill in analysis,
it does not come through great learning,
and it is beyond the scope of academics.

The nonthought created by stopping thought,
however deep and strong it may be,
is a great obscuration that prevents the birth of wisdom.

The spontaneous arising of realization's wisdom
certainly does not come
through desire or acquisition,
through being skilled or unskilled in analysis,
through great or little learning,
through wisdom or stupidity,
through good or bad experiences,
through intense or weak efforts, and so on.

It comes through relying upon a guru
and through your own merit.

"Relying upon a guru" means that
you receive it by pleasing a realized guru.
"Through your own merit" means that wisdom
comes to those predisposed through former training.

Therefore, as the wisdom of realization
is acquired on the path of blessing,
it is experienced by those who have faith,
it arises within those who have veneration,
and it is realized by those who are trained.
Diligence is a help in all of these.
It is the worthy ones with the highest capability who see
    wisdom.
The minds of those only skilled in words can't
    comprehend it.

The nondual realization that worthy individuals have
comes through the blessing of a sublime guru:
The dharmakaya arises from the middle of realization,
nonduality arises from the middle of the mind,
wisdom arises from the middle of the afflictions,
and realization arises from the middle of experiences.

The delusion of dualism will completely vanish,
as when a sleeping man wakes up.
On meeting nondual wisdom you awake and think,
"Oh! It's been here all along,
but I hadn't realized it before!

Nondual wisdom: what a joy!
My previous conduct: oh, so shameful!
It's realizing and not realizing it
that differentiates samsara from nirvana.
Up until now, before this realization,
I was like a man who was just
asleep and dreaming dreams:
I dreamed that I wandered in the ocean of samsara.
I dreamed that I suffered in the hells and so on.
I dreamed that, troubled, I turned to the guru.
I dreamed that I practiced his instructions.
I dreamed that experiences arose in my mind.
I dreamed that the luminosity arose as the dharmakaya.
I dreamed that the darkness of thought was dispelled.
I dreamed that there was no separation between
    meditation and post-meditation.
I dreamed that realization arose.
I dreamed that objectless compassion arose
toward beings without realization.
I dreamed that I attained the supreme mahamudra
and that my form kayas spontaneously accomplished the
    benefit of beings."

When you suddenly wake from that sleep,
there was no suffering of samsara,
there was no turning to the guru because you were
    troubled,
there was no practicing his instructions,
there was no arising of experiences in the mind,
there was no arising of luminosity as the dharmakaya,
there was no dispelling the darkness of thoughts,

there was no remaining in nonthought,
there was no arising of wisdom's realization,
there was neither beings nor compassion,
there was neither enlightenment nor attainment,
there was neither beings nor benefiting them,
there was neither truth nor falsity.

They were nothing but dream appearances.
Where did the samsara that you dreamed of
come from and where did it go?
Where did nirvana, the elimination of samsara,
come from and where did it go?
They and everything else were dream phenomena.
Where did they come from and where did they go?

It is the same as when a great king,
without leaving his throne for an instant,
in an illusion sits on a horse that runs away,
crossing many mountain passes and valleys.
Many months and years go by,
and he experiences all kinds of happiness and sorrow,
all without ever leaving his throne,
and without even the morning having passed by.

In the instant when realization arises,
when there is that great wisdom,
you comprehend the nature of all phenomena,
without becoming conceited by thinking, "I comprehend."
The nondual wisdom becomes manifest,
yet you don't become conceited by thinking, "It has
    manifested to me."

You are liberated from the three realms and from
    the Hinayana,
yet you don't become conceited by thinking, "I'm liberated."

In the instant that you realize nonduality,
you have certainty that all appearances and sounds are
    mind,
so that the Aspectarian doctrine is made manifest.
You have certainty in the clarity of the mind,
so that the Non-Aspectarian doctrine is made manifest.
You know self-knowing to be like an illusion,
so that the Illusion doctrine is perfected.
You know illusion to be empty,
so that the Utterly Nonabiding doctrine is perfected.

Emptiness arises as bliss
so that the view of nondual union is perfected.
That union has nonattention,
so that the mahamudra is made manifest
but without any identification through thinking, "It has
    manifested."

This wisdom through realization
does not come from anywhere,
does not go anywhere,
and does not reside anywhere.

The wisdom of realization and what it realizes
both dissolve into the nonconceptual essence of
    phenomena
without the arrogance of identifying it as the essence.

Now, remain within the equality that is like space.
Truly look at that which is true
and makes all thought and words meaningless.
When you truly see, you will be liberated.

The children have become tired
of the games that I have played.
If there is anything, offer it to the guru.
If there isn't anything, let the mind relax.

That is the gradualist's process of development.

In the indeterminates' process of development,
they gain stability, experiences, and realization.
An exceptional realization may arise first,
but that realization will be unstable, like waves.
They may sometimes have experiences and
sometimes have stability, in no certain order.
They are able to have both higher and lower experiences.

For the immediate kind of individuals,
experience, realization, and stability
arise simultaneously, without meditation,
as soon as a guru, who has the essence of realization,
teaches the instructions to them
or simply looks at their minds.

Whether their experiences increase or decrease,
their realization remains unchanged,
just as a tree remains unchanged
even though a monkey climbs up and down it;

just as the sky remains unchanged
even though rainbows appear or disappear in it;
just as the depths of the ocean do not change
whether waves rise or cease upon its surface.
It doesn't matter what experiences come or go
in the mind that is the natural presence of the dharmakaya.

If those who have clear experiences
do not blend those experiences with realization,
they will be like lamp flames in the midst of a tempest,
which will be ruinous for beginners.

For meditators who have gained stability,
everything, whether good or bad, will be an aid.
So, beginners, don't be afraid.

When a lamp is tiny,
even a faint breeze will extinguish it.
When a great fire blazes in a forest,
any strong wind will only increase it.

Meditators who don't have stability
may have occasional realizations,
but they have to feed the torch of realization
with the dry wood of experiences
while too much damp wood will extinguish it.

However high your realizations,
if your stability and experiences are not stable,

if you have no control over your own mind,
the afflictions—your enemies—will capture you.

That is like when an important man,
seized by enemies and held captive by weapons,
is on the road that leads home
but is not free to follow it.

Therefore, it's essential to maintain the torch of realization
through having stable experiences.
If you don't have control over your own mind,
you will lose the confidence of realization.

It's not in the mouth of someone who's all talk.
Be careful all you meditators,
for talking counteracts experiences.

Meditation and Post-Meditation
Meditation and post-meditation
doesn't mean "sitting down" and "standing up."

The beginner's meditation
is unwavering one-pointedness
upon any positive object whatsoever;
whether sitting or moving around, it's meditation.
If they don't remain one-pointed
and become lost in thought,
though they meditate on a cushion, it's post-meditation.

The meditation of realizing your own mind
is known as the successive four yogas.

The one-pointed yoga arises
when you realize the characteristics of your own mind
as unceasing emptiness and clarity, without center or
    edge,
like the middle of pure space.
That pure and vivid state
is the meditation of the first yoga.

When thoughts arise within that state,
even if you're meditating on a cushion, it's post-meditation.
If you remain in that pure, vivid clarity and emptiness,
whether you're talking, moving, or sitting,
you remain in the state of meditation.

The yoga of nonelaboration arises
when you realize the essence of your own mind
as a continuity of knowing, free from conceptual
    elaboration,
in which your own mind is the dharmakaya,
without birth or cessation, adoption or rejection.
That is the meditation of the second yoga.

When you remain in that meditation,
whether you're moving, sitting, or talking,
you remain in the state of meditation.
If you become distracted by the elaboration of concepts,
even if you're meditating on a cushion, it's post-meditation.

The yoga of one taste arises
when you realize the character of your own mind,
when you realize that the multiplicity of samsara and nirvana
arises from your mind, which is the dharmakaya free from
    conceptual elaboration.

The entire array of thought and nonthought,
appearances and no appearance, resting and no resting,
empty and not empty, clarity and no clarity,
are all one taste in the luminosity of the dharmakaya.

You see no appearances that are not the dharmakaya.
You see no thought that is not luminosity.

When the mind has that realization of equal taste,
it is the meditation of the third yoga.

While there is that natural mind,
whether you're running, jumping, or talking,
you remain in the state of meditation.
When you don't have the natural mind,
even if you're meditating on a cushion,
    it's post-meditation.

The yoga of nonmeditation arises
when the nature of knowing has no basis.
The practitioner has nothing to meditate on;
there is no meditator, only a state of evenness.

You will know what is meant by
"Buddhahood, with its three kayas

and five wisdoms, is complete in me."
You will have complete certainty that this itself
is the accomplishment of mahamudra.
You will not be conceited, thinking,
"I have attained the primordially present accomplishment!"
There will be neither mindfulness nor the absence of
     mindfulness.
There will be neither attention nor nonattention.
There will be neither one taste nor the absence of one taste.

There are no stages of meditation and post-meditation
in that self-sustaining knowledge of nonduality.
There is no death and there is no birth
in the continuous presence of knowing and emptiness.

A garuda's powers are already complete within the egg;
as soon as it hatches, it flies into the sky.
The qualities of the three kayas are already complete
     within the mind;
as soon as the body's trap is destroyed, they will benefit
     others.
When this nonmeditation arises,
there are no stages of meditation and post-meditation.

However high your realization,
while you are still familiarizing yourself with it,
there will still be stages of meditation and post-meditation,
there will still be mindfulness and the absence of
     mindfulness,
and there will still be distraction and the absence of
     distraction.

When you have completed the process of familiarization,
that is called *nonmeditation*,
where there are no stages of meditation and
    post-meditation,
there is nothing but a continuous state of meditation.
The mind of natural realization is present,
so whether you are moving about, sitting, or lying down,
whether you are sleeping or dreaming,
whether you are talking or eating,
there is nothing but meditation.

It is the jewel that naturally fulfills all needs and wishes.
It is the sun that naturally has light.
It is the yoga of constant meditation.
It is called manifest nonduality.

In the post-meditation of one-pointedness,
things appear to be solid
but are meditated upon as illusions.

In the post-meditation of nonelaboration,
things sometimes appear as illusions
and sometimes they appear to be solid,
but they are meditated upon as the dharmakaya.

In the post-meditation of the one-taste phase,
things arise as the dharmakaya when there is
    mindfulness,
but there are brief periods of solidity, when there is no
    mindfulness.

In nonmeditation, both meditation
and post-meditation are nothing but the dharmakaya,
and the two form kayas appear to others.

It's not in the mouth of someone who's all talk.
It's not in a mouth that boasts empty words.
Don't keep yourself in the dark!
When there is nonmeditation,
whether you are asleep or not, there is clarity.
Whether you are analyzing or not,
whether you have mindfulness or not,
there is clearly the dharmakaya, with no self or others.
Without any thought of making an effort,
Objectless compassion arises spontaneously.

Until you reach that level,
You are in grave danger of deceiving yourself
with a nonmeditation that's just clinging to empty talk.

Therefore, worthy meditators,
until you reach the level of nonmeditation,
honor the guru and accumulate merit.
If you are not deceived by clinging to empty talk,
your accumulation of merit will never let you down.
That is the heart advice of the realized ones.

As for being with others or being in solitude,
if you always have the wisdom of the dharmakaya,
are free from attachment to duality,
and are not overcome by the eight worldly concerns,

you will always be in solitude, even though you wander
    through a crowd.
However, if you have attachment to duality,
have ups and downs, and so on,
you are always in a crowd, even when you're in solitude.

Therefore, whether in solitude or with others,
always have the realization of nonduality,
don't go through ups and downs,
and prize having no attachment to anything.

The distinction between solitude and company,
between meditation and post-meditation, and so on,
are taught with the intention of guiding
those individuals who are beginners.
Ultimately, there are no such dualities
as solitude and company, meditation and post-meditation.

Why is that? Because the mind
is the innate dharmakaya
and appearances are the innate light of the dharmakaya,
just like a lamp's flame and its light.

Dharmakaya is the nature of knowing;
it can't possibly have discontinuity or fluctuation,
so how could there be meditation and post-meditation?
Who can deny the absence of meditation and
    post-meditation
in a meditator who has this enduring realization?
That is why they cannot be judged like ordinary individuals.

You may have experiences or realizations and think you
    are special,
but no matter how good the experiences are,
liberation is impossible without realization;
no matter how high the realizations are,
without compassion, they will be the śravaka path.

Even if you have experiences and samadhis
within the four dhyanas, and so on,
if you have the great fault of being without realization,
those experiences will cease, and afterward
you will fall into the three lower existences and so on
and experience unendurable suffering; think about that!

All experiences are composite;
everything composite is impermanent and will end.
Therefore, have no attachment to experiences
and realize nondual wisdom.

This nonabiding nirvana
is solely the province of realization.
Mentally fabricated nonduality,
which is what great scholars realize,
is solely the province of thought.

The nonduality that arises within
is nothing but the blessing of the guru.
The faithful who have veneration for the guru
develop the certainty of realization within themselves.
What does someone who just analyzes have?
Even I have understood it as words, too.

When realization arises in your mind,
examine to see whether it can withstand negative factors.
If someone on your right is swinging an axe at you
and saying all kinds of unpleasant things to you,
while someone on your left offers you the aroma of
 sandalwood
and respectfully says all kinds of pleasant thing to you,
if while you're having this experience,
you have no happiness or suffering, no like or dislike,
without having to make an effort to deal with it,
then you're ready to perform crazy behavior in public.

However, if you have no faith or if it's unstable,
if you haven't gained unimpeded powers,
and you publicly carry out the secretly taught conduct,
you will bring yourself and others to ruin.

When you have gained unimpeded powers,
such as various kinds of clairvoyance,
some of which may possibly be of benefit to others,
don't distinguish between secret and public conduct.

The venerable Mila taught that
the ten virtuous actions are not to be performed,
that the ten bad actions are not be abandoned,
and that you should rest in natural relaxation.

The venerable Loro taught that
the powerful, high, Three Jewels
are completely present in a state of devotionless knowing
in which there is nothing that can be called "going for refuge."

These viewpoints of those venerable ones
are as clear as a butter lamp in a vase
to me, the beggar monk from Shang,
and to all my realized vajra siblings.

But if I explain it, you will find it hard to understand,
for it's experienced only by those in whom it has
	spontaneously arisen,
by those who have faith, by those who have pleased their
	gurus
and whose blessing has entered into their hearts.

I am not going to describe the "all-victorious" conduct,
the "great meditation" conduct, or any of the others,
as I think that it would take too long;
since you can read about them within the ocean of
	supreme tantras,
I don't have to write too much here.

Perform the appropriate conduct at the appropriate
	time.
Avoid senseless behavior and empty chatter.
Practice without being too tight or too loose.
Maintain a view that is free of partiality.
Have a conduct that is free of artifice.
Have compassion that is without bias.
Meditate free from distraction.
Then there will be unceasing good qualities
and the accomplishment of unending benefit for beings.

If, without the realization of nonduality,

you could be liberated by
deliberately senseless behavior—
regarding enemies and friends, and gold and clods of
    earth, as the same,
and having no regard for respectability or reputation—
then why don't little children become liberated?

If, without the realization of nonduality,
you could be liberated by disregard for what is proper,
then every lunatic would be liberated.

If, without the realization of nonduality,
you could be liberated by disregard for cleanliness,
then every dog and pig would be liberated.

If, without the realization of nonduality,
you could be liberated by skillful conduct,
then every new bride would be liberated.

If you could be liberated by a natural relaxation
that lacks the realization of nonduality,
then every idiot would be liberated.

If you do have the realization of nonduality,
then however you act, whether wild or precise, you will
    be liberated.

If you don't have the realization of nonduality,
whether your conduct is precise or wild, you will be in
    bondage.

If you are permeated by impartial compassion,
whatever you do will be the supreme path.
If you are not permeated by impartial compassion,
whatever you do will be the inferior path.

Impartiality

The true nature in that view,
and all other qualities, such as meditation,
conduct, commitment, and result,
are all manifestations of your own mind.

The mind is a state of clear self-knowing.
That clarity has an empty nature,
like space; it cannot be divided.
There are no directions, center, or limits to be identified.

There is no duality of viewer and viewed
in the nature of the mind.
Therefore, there is no view and no realization.

There is no duality of meditator and object of meditation.
Therefore, there is no meditation and no experience.

There is no duality of familiarizer and familiarized.
Therefore, there is no familiarization and no absence of
    familiarization.

There is no duality of someone distracted and an object
    of distraction.
Therefore, there is no nondistraction and no distraction.

There is no duality of performer of conduct and per-
    formed conduct.
Therefore, there is no conduct and nothing that is
    performed.

There is no duality of someone who attains and something
    attained.
Therefore, there is no accomplishment and no attainment.

There is no duality of cause and result,
just like the center of empty space.
Therefore, there is no generation and no ripening.

There is no obscuration and no purification
in the mind that is primordially empty;
it is the immaterial inseparability of knowing and
    emptiness.
Therefore, there is no wisdom and no ignorance.

The meditators who thus know,
in the luminous essence of the mind,
the equality of view, meditation,
conduct, commitment, and result
have no attachment to a viewer and a viewed.
Therefore, they are the kings of attachment-free view.

They have no attachment to a meditator and object of
    meditation.
Therefore, they are the kings of attachment-free
    meditation.

They have no attachment to a performer of conduct and
    a performed conduct.
Therefore, they are the kings of attachment-free conduct.

They have no attachment to someone who attains and
    something attained.
Therefore, they are the kings of attachment-free result.

The White Panacea
In the instant that you realize your own mind,
all good qualities, without exception,
are simultaneously completed without having to accom-
    plish them.

The three kayas are primordially, naturally present
in the nature of the mind, which is like space;
the Jewel of the Buddha is completely within it.

The nature of the mind is free of elaboration, free of
    desire;
the Jewel of the Dharma is complete within it.

Its nature is birthless and irreversible,
with the variety of thoughts arising as its companions;
the Jewel of the Sangha is complete within it.

Even the Three Jewels
are complete in your own mind's knowing.
Therefore, there is no need to seek refuge elsewhere;
the definitive refuge is complete in it.

In the nature of the mind, which is without elaboration,
there is no basis for desire and selfishness.
Therefore, the aspiration bodhicitta is complete in it.

Everything is understood to be an illusion,
so that objectless compassion arises
and benefiting others is naturally present.
Therefore, the bodhicitta of engagement is complete
    in that.

In the nature of the mind, which is like space,
there is freedom from all fixation and attachment.
Therefore, the perfection of generosity is complete in that.

It is perfectly pure of the stains of concepts.
Therefore, the perfection of conduct is complete in that.

There is no fear of emptiness and the seeds of anger are
    vanquished.
Therefore, the perfection of patience is complete in that.

The union of knowing and emptiness is never interrupted.
Therefore, the perfection of diligence is complete in that.

One-pointedness is primordially, naturally present.
Therefore, the perfection of meditation is complete
    in that.

There is spontaneous liberation from the concepts of
    wrong views.
Therefore, the perfection of wisdom is complete in that.

Everything that appears arises as companions.
Therefore, the great method, the great accumulation of
    merit, is complete in that.

The meaning of nonduality is realized.
Therefore, the great accumulation of wisdom is complete
    in that.

In the nature of the mind, which is like space,
there are no stains whatsoever from the body.
Therefore, the supreme vase empowerment is complete
    in that.

There is primordial purity from the stains of speech.
Therefore, the supreme secret empowerment is complete
    in that.

There is no location for the stains of the mind.
Therefore, the supreme empowerment of the prajña's
    wisdom is complete in that.

There is no location for stains that come equally from
    body, speech, and mind.
Therefore, the supreme fourth empowerment is complete
    in that.

The naturally clear knowing is unceasing
and appears as every kind of body, color, and insignia.
Therefore, every kind of generation stage is complete in
    that.

The clarity has no conceptual identification.
Therefore, the completion stage is complete in that.

The superior realization of your own mind as
nondual luminosity is the path of seeing,
its unbroken continuity is the path of meditation,
its effortlessness is the path of complete attainment.

Not being limited by anything is the supreme sign of heat.
Therefore the signs of heat on the paths and levels are
    complete in that.

Being nothing whatsoever: that is the dharmakaya.
Appearing as anything whatsoever: that is the
    nirmanakaya.
All that appears is enjoyed (*sambhoga*) as the
    dharmakaya.
Therefore, the resultant three kayas are complete in that.

As there is no partiality in self-knowing,
which is like space, the view is complete in that.
As there is no attachment to objects of perception,
    meditation is complete in that.
As there is no adoption or rejection, conduct is complete
    in that.
As there is no loss, commitment is complete in that.
As there is natural presence, the result is complete in that.

There are no three times, there is no before and after,
in the empty luminosity of the mind.

For as long as there is fixation upon a self,
there will be view, meditation, conduct, result, and
	commitment,
and there will be karma and the ripening of karma.
So it's essential to avoid bad actions and accumulate
	merit.

Colophon

Nowadays, in these evil times, it is rare for Dharma
	practitioners
to tame their beings and speech with study.
Though skilled in words, they don't realize their meaning,
so that arrogance and quarrels increase.

We should follow and accomplish the meaning
taught by the venerable gurus of the practice lineage,
completely eliminating pride, and so on,
and realize the meaning, which fulfills the purpose of
	scripture and logic.

Tilopa did not speak
a single word to Naropa,
yet all scripture, logic, and instruction
became complete in Naropa's mind.

Therefore, this chattering of mine,
though eloquent in its expression of humility and so on,
has the faults of contradiction, connection, calculation,
	and repetition,
and it is comprised of empty, unexamined words.

Nevertheless, there is the faintest possibility that
when passed on to my pupils it will help them.
That is the reason why I've written this.
If a single word of it contradicts
scripture, logic, or the instructions, may my head
    split open!

This is the extent of beggar monk Shang's realization.
I wrote it on the urging of Marpa, my attendant,
In front of the Pangbu Thul cliffs.

Do not show this to people, or you will accumulate bad
    karma.

This has been my description of the words of the Buddha,
    their commentaries, the viewpoints of the sublime
    gurus, and my own realization.

8: Guidance in Zazen— Those Who Greatly Realize Delusion Are Buddhas

by Shohaku Okumura,
adapted by Josh Bartok
from the book *Realizing Genjokoan*

Delusion is not some fixed thing within our minds that, if eliminated, will be replaced by enlightenment.

The world we live in is the world we create, based on how our mind encounters the myriad dharmas. We cannot prevent our mind from creating the world as it does, but it is possible to realize that the world of our creation does not reflect true reality. Practicing with this realization, and letting go of rigid belief in the narratives and preferences of our minds, is opening the hand of thought.

Within consciousness, reality is always distorted; we don't see things as they are, and that is delusion. We take our distorted ideas and desires, and move toward the world, trying to *find* reality. We try to *see* reality with our minds, abilities, willpower, and effort. All of this is delusion.

To practice is to awaken to the self that is part of all things. The subject of practice is not the personal self but all beings. It is not we who engage in our practice, but rather it is Buddha who carries out Buddha's practice through us.

Zazen is not a matter of individual actions or experiences emerging from individual willpower or effort. Zazen is not a practice that makes beings into buddhas; zazen itself is Buddha's practice.

Zazen enables us to see clearly that we are part of the world, part of nature, part of Buddha. There is no separate individual who practices zazen and becomes enlightened. We actualize the self that is connected with all dharmas. We don't personally become a buddha, but rather we awaken to the reality that, from the beginning, we are living Buddha's life. Enlightenment is not the self awakening to reality but zazen awakening to zazen, Dharma awakening to Dharma, Buddha awakening to Buddha.

This is the meaning of "practice and enlightenment are one."

———

No matter how hard we practice, our motivation for practice is always based in some amount of self-centeredness. The act of truly seeing this self-centeredness is itself Buddha. To awaken to the reality of our delusion is itself Buddha.

To realize delusion is to be a buddha. Awakening to the incompleteness of our practice and returning to our path is the meaning of repentance, of atonement.

In zazen, we let go of our narrow, limited, karmic selves and become one with the total, interpenetrating whole that is absolute reality. We can never see this absolute reality as an object of our discriminating minds, but we are naturally a part of it. We cannot be an observer of absolute reality because we ourselves are part of its total movement.

Even amid delusion, we are still living within absolute, universal reality; and even though we are living within absolute, universal reality, we are still deluded as limited, karmic selves. This is the reality of human life.

In zazen, it is not the "I"—the limited karmic self—that awakens to reality; rather, it is the reality of the universe that is itself practicing and manifesting reality. Great realization actualizes great realization through our practice.

Zazen is not a method of correcting the distortion of our fabricated conceptual maps but rather is the act of letting go of all maps and sitting down on the ground of reality. Letting go is at once the complete rejection of any formation arising in our limited karmic mind and the acceptance of all formations as mere secretions of the mind.

We let thoughts come up, and we let them go away. We neither negate nor affirm anything in zazen. Zazen goes beyond, and yet includes, complete rejection and complete acceptance of thought.

When we sit in the upright posture, keeping the eyes open, breathing through the nose, and letting go of mental formations, reality manifests itself. This is *genjokoan*, the actualization of reality. At this time, only manifesting reality exists, and manifesting reality includes our delusions.

Practicing in this way helps us understand that our map of the world is biased and incomplete, and this understanding allows us to be flexible. Practicing in this way broadens our view, and this broadened view allows us to be better at working in harmony with others.

In zazen, there is no way we can judge ourselves because we cannot step outside our mental formations into true reality. True reality is beyond such judgments. There is no way to conceive of being a buddha or of being enlightened, yet without trying to be a buddha, and without trying to become enlightened, in zazen we keep settling more and more deeply into immeasurable reality.

Zazen itself is this immeasurable reality.

9: Instructions for an Ordinary Symphony

by David Rynick,
from the book *This Truth Never Fails*

Gather ten thousand people.

Give each person two leaves.

(Make sure you have a variety of leaf shapes and sizes—some round and some angular, some the size of quarters and some the size of a pro basketball player's hands.)

Spread these people out randomly in a quarter mile radius.

Have them wait for your signal.

Gather several hundred cars and drivers.

(Again, variation is most essential.)

Have them wait out of sight—half of them wait to the east of the house and half wait to the west.

And use other vehicles too—mostly cars, but large trucks too—and make sure some of the trucks are filled with something heavy (we need that deep rumbling bass as they accelerate from the red light).

Have them all wait for your signal.

Now give the signal. (It should be grand and unmistakable.)

Leaf people: hit your two leaves against each other. Vary the rhythm and timing of your leaf striking. It must come and go like the wind. Let yourself feel the timing.

Drivers: start your vehicles at specific intervals then drive by in front of the house. Mix in the occasional truck. Come singly and in clumps. (Pay attention to the traffic light nearby. The idling is important.) And truck drivers: don't forget that lovely loud downshift to decelerate. (We need variation to enhance the softer sound of smaller cars.)

And don't forget the birds.

Position some in the trees nearby with loud squawks and have some so far away you can barely hear them.

Now shake the leaves. Have the rustling start on one side of the space and then go to the other. Have that indescribably soft sound begin and end quickly—then have it go on longer and slowly diminish.

Now a car.

Now several birds.

Have them seem to be engaging in a conversation. Make it be of some importance.

More leaves hitting against each other.

Now the slamming of a car door and the starting of an engine.

Don't stop—keep this music going night and day, constantly vary the timing and the intensity.

We've all been waiting so long to hear this unrivaled masterpiece.

Index of Topics

Numbers below indicate "dose numbers" rather than page numbers.
A number that starts with an "s" indicates a SUPPLEMENT.

Index of Names Cited

*Numbers below indicate "dose numbers" rather than page numbers.
A number that starts with an "s" indicates a supplement.*

Bibliography and Index
by Book Cited

All titles below published by Wisdom Publications, Boston.

Numbers below indicate "dose numbers" rather than page numbers. A number that starts with an "s" indicates a SUPPLEMENT.

The Art of Disappearing: The Buddha's Path to Lasting Joy. Ajahn Brahm. 2011. [168, 253, 326]

The Attention Revolution: Unlocking the Power of the Focused Mind. B. Alan Wallace. 2006. [5, 15, 22, 95, 156, 175, 195]

Awakening the Kind Heart: How to Meditate on Compassion. Kathleen McDonald. 2010. [3, 21, 119, 194, 248, 307, 337]

The Beginner's Guide to Insight Meditation. Revised Edition. Arinna Weisman and Jean Smith. 2010. [71, 136, 211, 280]

The Best of Inquiring Mind: 25 Years of Dharma, Drama, and Uncommon Insight. Gene Reeves. Edited by Barbara Gates and Wes Nisker. 2008. [29, 58, 94, 128, 155, 187, 220, 252, 284, 316, 349]

The Blue Poppy and the Mustard Seed: A Mother's Story of Loss and Hope. Kathleen Willis Morton. 2008. [116, 235]

The Book of Mu: Essential Writings on Zen's Most Important Koan. Edited by James Ishmael Ford and Melissa Myozen Blacker. 2011. [25, 77, 138, 207, 255, 303]

Buddha at the Apocalypse: Awakening from a Culture of Destruction. Kurt Spellmeyer. 2010. [322]

Buddhism and Psychotherapy Across Cultures: Essays on Theories and Practices. Edited by Mark Unno. 2006. [19, 42, 158, 259, 274]

429

The Lotus Sutra: A Contemporary Translation of a Buddhist Classic. Translated and introduced by Gene Reeves. 2008. [97, 159, 228, 294, 348]

Mahamudra and Related Instructions: Core Teachings of the Kagyu Schools. Translated by Peter Alan Roberts. 2011. [8, 30, 67, 103, 130, 148, 196, 261, 319, 357]

Mahamudra—The Moonlight: Quintessence of Mind and Meditation. Dakpo Tashi Namgyal. Translated and annotated by Lobsang P. Lhalungpa. 2006. [117, 318]

Making Zen Your Own: Giving Life to Twelve Key Golden Age Ancestors. Janet Jiryu Abels. 2012. [78, 164, 247]

Meditation and Relaxation in Plain English. Bob Sharples. 2006. [1, 23, 47, 81, 133, 153, 242, 341]

The Meditator's Atlas: A Roadmap of the Inner World. Matthew Flickstein. 2007. [39, 90, 127, 178, 226, 265, 309]

Meditation on the Nature of Mind. The Dalai Lama, Khonton Peljor Lhundrub, and Jose Ignacio Cabezon. 2011. [215]

The Middle Way: Faith Grounded in Reason. The Dalai Lama. Translated by Thupten Jinpa. 2009. [64, 102, 171, 206, 266, 302]

Mindful Monkey, Happy Panda. Story by Lauren Alderfer. Illustrations by Kerry Lee MacLean. 2011. [80]

Mindfulness, Bliss, and Beyond: A Meditator's Handbook. Ajahn Brahm. 2006. [38, 63, 76, 89, 162, 182, 191, 281, 334]

Mindful Politics: A Buddhist Guide to Making the World a Better Place. Edited by Melvin McLeod. 2006. [18, 52, 55, 70, 91, 111, 131, 221, 251, 271, 321]

Mindful Teaching and Teaching Mindfulness: A Guide for Anyone Who Teaches Anything. Deborah Schoeberlein with Suki Sheth. 2009. [54, 109, 170, 231, 290, 351]

Mindful Therapy: A Guide for Therapists and Helping Professionals. Thomas Bien. 2006. [43, 73, 93, 124, 173, 203, 232, 263]

The Mindful Writer: Noble Truths of the Writing Life. Dinty W. Moore. 2012. [144, 197, 286]

Minding What Matters: Psychotherapy and the Buddha Within. Robert Langan. 2006. [51, 82, 135]

Mixing Minds: The Power of Relationship in Psychology and Buddhism. Pilar Jennings. 2010. [141, 328]

Momentary Buddhahood: Mindfulness and the Vajrayana Path. Anyen Rinpoche. 2009. [86, 181, 269, 360]

Moon by the Window: The Calligraphy and Zen Insights of Shodo Harada. Shodo Harada. 2011. [60, 134, 199, 272, 344]

Natural Perfection: Longchenpa's Radical Dzogchen. Longchen Rabjam. Translated by Keith Dowman. 2010. [104, 297]

Never Turn Away: The Buddhist Path Beyond Hope and Fear. Rigdzin Shikpo. 2007. [169, 289]

No River to Cross: Trusting the Enlightenment That's Always Right Here. Daehaeng Sunim. 2007. [79, 160, 241, 320]

Nothing Is Hidden. Barry Magid. 2013. [37, 41, 257, 285]

One City: A Declaration of Interdependence. Ethan Nichtern. 2007. [279]

One Hundred Days of Solitude: Losing Myself and Finding Grace on a Zen Retreat. Jane Dobisz. 2007. [36, 99, 165, 223, 278]

Pointing Out the Great Way: The Stages of Meditation in the Mahamudra Tradition. Daniel P. Brown. 2006. [4]

Realizing Genjokoan: The Key to Dogen's Shobogenzo. Shohaku Okumura. 2010. (s8)

Razor-Wire Dharma: A Buddhist Life in Prison. Calvin Malone. 2008. [225, 355]

Saltwater Buddha: A Surfer's Quest to Find Zen on the Sea. Jaimal Yogis. 2009. [149, 256, 329]

Sex and the Spiritual Teacher: Why It Happens, When It's a Problem, and What We All Can Do. Scott Edelstein. 2011. [11, 180]

A Song for the King: Saraha on Mahamudra Meditation. Khenchen Thrangu Rinpoche. Edited by Michele Martin. 2006. [44, 154, 254]

The Stories of the Lotus Sutra. Gene Reeves. 2010. [40]

Together Under One Roof: Making a Home of the Buddha's Household. Lin Jensen. 2008. [16, 49, 65, 84, 122, 150, 179, 210, 246, 292, 342]

This Truth Never Fails: A Zen Memoir in Four Seasons. David Rynick. 2012. [415]

12 Steps on the Buddha's Path: Bill, Buddha, and We—A Spiritual Journey of Recovery. Laura S. 2006. [48, 72, 92, 212]

The Two Truths Debate: Tsongkhapa and Gorampa on the Middle Way. Sonam Thakchoe. 2007. [31]

Unlearning the Basics: A New Way of Understanding Yourself and the World. Rishi Sativihari. 2010. [145, 217, 283, 345]

Unlimiting Mind: The Radically Experiential Psychology of Buddhism. Andrew Olendzki. 2010. [7, 32, 62, 75, 101, 114, 139, 163, 192, 219, 250, 277, 305, 323, 346]

Upside-Down Zen. Susan Murphy. 2006. [27, 125, 143, 176, 201, 213, 233, 244, 267, 282, 295, 313, 335, 354]

Walking the Way: 81 Zen Encounters with the Tao Te Ching. Robert Meikyo Rosenbaum. 2013. [239]

Warrior-King of Shambhala: Remembering Chogyam Trungpa. Jeremy Hayward. 2007. [26, 291]

Wholesome Fear: Transforming Your Anxiety About Impermanence and Death. Lama Zopa Rinpoche and Kathleen McDonald. 2010. [359]

Wild Chickens and Petty Tyrants: 108 Metaphors for Mindfulness. Arnie Kozak. 2009. [59, 126, 186, 236, 304, 356]

Wisdom Wide and Deep: A Practical Handbook for Mastering Jhana and Vipassana. Shaila Catherine. 2011. [35, 330]

434

Women Practicing Buddhism: American Experiences. Edited by Peter N. Gregory and Susanne Mrozik. 2007. [85, 332]

The World Is Made of Stories. David R. Loy. 2010. [2, 88, 177, 214, 287, 363]

You Are Not Here: And Other Works of Buddhist Fiction. Edited by Keith Kachtick. 2006. [365]

Zen Master WHO? A Guide to the People and Stories of Zen. James Ishmael Ford. 2006. [20, 83, 140, 205, 262, 325]

Zen Questions: Zazen, Dogen, and the Spirit of Creative Inquiry. Taigen Dan Leighton. 2011. [106, 198, 260, 361]

Zen Radicals, Rebels, and Reformers. Perle Besserman and Manfred B. Steger. 2011. [331]

Zen Under the Gun: Four Zen Masters from Turbulent Times. Translated by J. C. Cleary. 2010. [137, 327]

Zen Women: Beyond Tea Ladies, Iron Maidens, and Macho Masters. Grace Schireson. 2009. [9, 96, 183, 275]

About the Editor

Josh Bartok, a Dharma heir of James Ishmael Ford, is one of the guiding teachers of Boundless Way Zen and the abbot of the Greater Boston Zen Center in Cambridge, Massachusetts. Additionally, he served as a senior editor at Wisdom Publications for over twelve years, having edited nearly two hundred books on myriad aspects of Buddhism.

About Wisdom Publications

Wisdom Publications is dedicated to offering works relating to and inspired by Buddhist traditions.

To learn more about us or to explore our other books, please visit our website at www.wisdompubs.org.

You can subscribe to our e-newsletter or request our print catalog online, or by writing to:

Wisdom Publications
199 Elm Street
Somerville, Massachusetts 02144 USA

You can also contact us at 617-776-7416 or by email at info@wisdompubs.org.

Wisdom is a nonprofit, charitable 501(c)(3) organization, and donations in support of our mission are tax deductible.

Wisdom Publications is affiliated with the Foundation for the Preservation of the Mahayana Tradition (FPMT).

Related Books

Saying Yes to Life (Even the Hard Parts)
by Ezra Bayda with Josh Bartok

Like a Yeti Catching Marmots:
A Little Treasury of Tibetan Proverbs
by Pema Tsewang Shastri and Josh Bartok

Daily Wisdom: 365 Buddhist Inspirations
edited by Josh Bartok

More Daily Wisdom: 365 Buddhist Inspirations
edited by Josh Bartok

Nightly Wisdom: Buddhist Inspirations
for Sleeping, Dreaming, and Waking Up
compiled by Gustavo Cutz
edited by Josh Bartok

Lama Zopa Rinpoche's *How to Be Happy*
edited by Josh Bartok and Ailsa Cameron

Lama Yeshe's *When the Chocolate Runs Out*
edited by Josh Bartok and Nicholas Ribush